THE ADOPTION EXPERIENCE
Stories and Commentaries

Steven L. Nickman

 B.C.H.S. LIBRARY BURLINGTON, N.J.

JULIAN MESSNER
New York

Copyright © 1985 by Steven L. Nickman

All rights reserved
including the right of reproduction
in whole or in part in any form.
Published by Julian Messner,
A Division of Simon & Schuster, Inc.
Simon & Schuster Building
Rockefeller Center
1230 Avenue of the Americas
New York, New York   10020

JULIAN MESSNER and colophon are
trademarks of Simon & Schuster, Inc.

"By the Winding River I" by Tu Fu, as
re-arranged for *The Adoption Experience*.
Kenneth Rexroth, ONE HUNDRED POEMS FROM THE
CHINESE. Copyright © 1971 by Kenneth Rexroth.
All Rights Reserved.
Reprinted by permission of
New Directions Publishing Corporation.

Manufactured in the United States of America

Library of Congress Cataloging in Publication Data

Nickman, Steven L.

The Adoption Experience

  Bibliography: p.
  Includes index.
  Summary: Presents various aspects of adoption
including interracial adoption, searching for birth
parents, and giving up a child for adoption. Also
discusses the feelings of the participants, the
provisions of the law, possible problems and their
solutions, and ways in which adopted people are
different or alike from those that are not adopted.
  1. Adoption—Juvenile literature. 2. Interracial
adoption—Juvenile literature. [1. Adoption] I. Title.
HV875.N45   1985   362.7'34   85-8957
ISBN: 0-671-50817-2

This book is dedicated to Russell and Peter, and

*to all the brave hurt angry kids
who use the love around them and the strength
inside them to get past their pain
and go on to be kind and generous, spreading
light where they go.*

CONTENTS

TO THE READER 9
WHAT DID YOU SAY YOUR NAME WAS? 13
JOANNA 46
THE ASSIGNMENT 69
HORMONES HAVE NO COLOR 89
THE GHOSTS IN THE BOX 108
SOMETHING DIED 139
LETTER TO AN UNKNOWN BABY 163

SUGGESTIONS FOR FURTHER READING 187
INDEX 189

ACKNOWLEDGMENTS

I am grateful to my wife and children and to my mother for encouragement during the writing of this book. I regret that my father, who was a pediatrician, cannot see it; he possessed much wisdom about children, and I hope some of it has been transmitted to these pages.

Many of my teachers, friends, colleagues, and patients have helped in various ways, knowingly or not; I am grateful to them, and to those members of my own profession who have helped me to know myself.

The published work of scholars such as David Kirk and Marshall Schechter was available when I needed it. Subsequently I came to know David and found him generous and encouraging.

Finally I owe a special debt to two people. Janet Chenery patiently and skillfully helped me turn the stories in this book from a series of rough pieces into something more worthy of publication. (My editor at Julian Messner, Jane Steltenpohl, picked up the stories and commentaries from there.) My son Russell provided the initial stimulus for the book, and throughout has supported my efforts enthusiastically. This book would not exist without him.

TO THE READER

Maybe you're adopted. Perhaps you have a brother or sister or friend who is. Or maybe you're just curious about the kinds of experience that many adopted kids have. Whatever the reason for your interest, this book is for you.

According to the best estimates, roughly 3 percent of American kids are adopted. About half of these are not related by blood to either of their adoptive parents. The rest were adopted by grandparents or other relatives, or by a stepparent after the divorce and remarriage of the parent with whom the child stayed.

Usually when people think of adoption, they picture the first group: boys and girls, men and women, who grew up with parents with whom they don't have a biological tie. It's these people that this book is directly about. But the other group is not completely distinct from the first; I think, for example, of a boy I know whose mother died. His father then remarried, and his stepmother adopted him legally, but not long afterward the couple split up, and the boy remains with his adoptive mother, who's not his blood relative.

Situations like this boy's are not terribly rare. And with the large numbers of divorced and remarried people in this country, there has come to be a huge number of kids who spend part or all of their time in a home where one of the parents is not their original father or mother—and where there are other kids (half-brothers and sisters, stepbrothers and sisters) who are only related through one parent or not related to them at all.

Families such as this are sometimes called *blended families*, but the typical adoptive family—the first group mentioned above—is a kind of blended family, too, in that it took something special (in this case the adoptive process) to bring them together. It's clear that there exists a whole range of family types that would have been considered unusual, or out of the mainstream, thirty or forty years ago, but which in these last decades of the twentieth century are becoming almost as common as the "classical" family setup: a husband and wife living with children who carry both parents' genes.

Change in social customs which affects the makeup of families is not new. For example, it is much less common than it used to be for grandparents to live in the same house with their grown children and their grandchildren. And families tend to have fewer children now than they did years ago.

There are reasons for these changes—but we need not be too concerned here with the reasons. Rather, this book was written for kids who are interested in how it *feels* to belong to a certain part of this large, nonmainstream group of families. To be specific, it is for anyone who's interested in what it's like to be adopted and wants to know about some of the special experiences adopted kids have.

There are seven stories in the book. Six are about adopted kids, and one tells about a young man and woman who are the birth parents of a baby who will be adopted. The stories are fictional—that is, none of them is directly based on the history of a particular boy or girl—but they illustrate some situations that are common for adopted kids and their families.

After each story you'll find a commentary. In these sections I've given some information that should help connect the story with the world outside the pages of this book. There's a lot about adoption that's sometimes not easy to understand, and the commentaries were added to help you with some of its more puzzling aspects. I haven't included a great deal about the history of adoption—because there seemed to be enough other things to write about, and because there are now good books available for kids who want to know how the ancient custom of adoption evolved into its present forms. (At the end of the book there's a list of additional readings for people who want to pursue the subject further.)

One final point: in the last paragraph I mentioned *forms* of adoption—in the plural. The reason is that adoption in America has undergone tremendous changes. Various forms of adoption coexist in America today. Certain kinds of kids and parents are being brought together now who would never have been considered as an adoptive unit thirty years ago. And the commonest form of adoption at that time—placement in early infancy—is considerably less common today. Yet one of today's patterns, the placement of older children and teenagers, is closer to what adoption was in Roman days!

This is an exciting time for people who are interested

in watching social change. But change can be troublesome and confusing, especially for a person who's right in the middle of it. And many adopted people feel troubled from time to time, whether they were placed "traditionally" as infants, or as older children in accordance with more recent adoptive customs.

This book was written for the reader's enjoyment, but also to provide useful information and to give comfort to those kids who think about adoption a lot and feel angry and sad, perhaps even abandoned. Some of them may discover that other people have feelings about adoption that they thought were theirs alone. I can assure you that although these are fictional stories, I didn't invent the feelings portrayed here.

Growing up is hard enough anyway. If this book can help a few people who have to deal with adoption on top of the rest of growing up, then writing it will have been well worth the effort.

WHAT DID YOU SAY YOUR NAME WAS?

The rain battered the tree under which Chris huddled. It was the height of the storm; at least it couldn't get any worse, he reflected. He was tired at the end of the day, and he hoped things would quiet down. Then, he figured, he could get some sleep, and his belongings would stay dry.

He'd brought clothes, food, a knife, compass, and canteen, and his wallet with identification, assorted cards and photos, and thirty dollars. And a notebook which he now opened; it was blank except for the first page. He looked at what he had written there a month before when he planned his trip:

COMEAU
Kingston
5/1/66

Comeau: looks like a French name, Chris thought. Well, Frenchies aren't so bad. Some of my best friends are French! And he tried to laugh, but it came out sounding forced. He pulled a comic book out of his pack and began reading about Spider-Man, and crawled into the sack. He thought about his bed back home in Toronto, and he thought about bears. Then he quickly thought about Toronto again and went to sleep.

Next morning Chris had a quick meal of bread and cheese washed down with rainwater. The sun was out and it was already warm. Before eight everything was stowed in his pack, and he headed east, parallel to Route 401 but keeping half a mile north of it. He didn't want to thumb; he was sure that by now his parents would have the police on his trail.

At this rate, Chris thought, he'd make Kingston in three more days, or two if he were lucky. On the way he hoped somehow to supplement the meager sum of money he'd been able to bring with him.

On the fifth day he walked into a Shell station in Napanee, twenty miles west of Kingston, and used their rest room to wash up. Then he asked about their HELP WANTED sign. The owner, a heavy, muscular man in his late thirties with the beginnings of a beer belly, looked Chris over silently for a moment and then asked, "Just passing through?"

Chris was prepared to explain himself. "I'm on my summer vacation, on a walking tour. Going to see my aunt and uncle in Gananoque." (The town he mentioned was east of Kingston; in case anyone tried to trace him, it would throw them off the scent.) "Just thought a little money'd come in handy. I could work for you three, four days, pumping gas, helping out in your snack bar. Even a week if you want. Then I'd be on my way. I'm a good worker; you wouldn't regret it."

"I could use some help, even temporary. It's the height of the tourist season, and two kids that was workin' for me decided they'd rather go fishin'. You have to be sixteen to work the pumps, though. How old are you?"

"Seventeen last month," Chris lied.

"Need a place to stay?"

Chris grinned. "It sure would help."

"Well then. My name's Tony Wilkes, and in that restaurant there's my wife and two of my kids workin'. I'll pay you twenty-five bucks a day and you can stay as long as we both think you should. There's a spare bed in the garage office you can use. There's a sink and shower in there, too."

Chris stayed five days. He knew the money he'd started out with wouldn't last long in Kingston, if he had to stay there longer than the week he counted on to accomplish his mission. He had every intention of being back in school in September and living in his old room, assuming that Mom and Pop didn't have him placed in the reformatory instead. But that, Chris pondered, was the chance he had to take.

With every day that passed at Tony's service station, Chris got more restless. On the fourth day he made a careless mistake at the cash register and short-changed a customer. Tony was pretty good about it. "You're an honest kid. I think you've just got your mind on somethin' else."

Chris said, "I guess you're right. I better be moving on tomorrow. Wouldn't want to make any more mistakes on the register!"—and he smiled. That night Tony's wife gave him his first home-cooked meal in more than a week, and he choked up a little when he saw her kiss their children good night.

Next morning Chris's mouth fell open as Tony handed him a hundred and forty dollars—"Fifteen for a bonus," Tony said. It was more money than he had ever seen at one time. And with a pang he thought, it's more than half my father's weekly paycheck.

He was in Kingston by early afternoon. On the way he'd gone over his plans. First he would walk around the center of town to learn where things were, so he could get around quickly if he had to. Then he'd locate the office he needed, and maybe the hospital, too. And he had to find a place to stay.

Lake Ontario looked the same in Kingston as it had in Toronto. I could have come here in a day and a half if I had a motorboat, he thought. But the town was small and had an old charm to it. Chris was relieved to see souvenir shops and tourists. On the streets and through the plate-glass windows of the restaurants he could see Americans, Indians, even Eskimos from the Territories; he would attract little notice in a town with a transient summer population.

He sat down on a bench in the little waterfront park and ate lunch from his pack. Nearby were some young children playing around a big modern sculpture. A striking looking girl around eighteen was watching them. She had long black hair, light blue eyes and a turned-up nose.

Half an hour later Chris knew her name and a lot more besides. What he was mainly after was the name of a place he could stay cheaply for a few days; Sally, who was a student at Queen's University, knew of several boarding-houses near the school that might serve his purpose. Changing his story from the one he had given Tony Wilkes, he'd told her he was in town to visit his beloved grandmother who was living in an old-age home. And Sally talked to him like the big sister he'd never had.

He cleaned himself up in the men's room of a service station and looked for Mrs. Sands's boardinghouse. There was a sign in front of the large old house: MEALS, LODGING, STUDENT ACCOMMODATIONS. Chris had no trouble taking a room.

He took a hot shower, washed his dirty clothes, and thought about his next step. If he went to the town offices, he figured he stood a chance of finding a sympathetic clerk; on the other hand, if he went to the hospital, he might get more detailed information, but he had no idea how to go about asking for it. Besides, he had a feeling that if theft were necessary, it might be easier in an office building than in a hospital . . .

Lying on the bed in his rented room, thinking, he soon dozed off. When he awoke it was after four. He hadn't realized he was so tired. Fragments of a dream went through his head; there was a piece about his mother, blotting her tear-filled eyes and telling his father, *I guess I won't be making scones for breakfast again, Howard.* Scones were Chris's favorite of all the things his mother baked. And then he remembered another fragment: there was a beautiful garden inside a stone wall that had no door in it, and Chris was butting his head again and again against the wall in a savage fury, trying to get in. Hateful officials approached him; they wore gray uniforms and their caps bore the legend BORDER GUARDS. They waved him away, but he ran from them and kept banging against the wall as though his head were a hammer.

And, sitting there now, he had a monstrous headache. His weeks of difficult travel and life in hiding seemed like a picnic excursion compared with what he was about to do, and he felt tired and worried. What if he failed? At best, he could return home and face his parents' anger for leaving them with nothing but a brief, vague note to indicate his plan.

Gone for a while. Fact-finding expedition. Don't worry.

Love,
Chris

At worst, he would be in legal trouble and found delinquent; his parents would have to go with him to the juvenile court. But either way, he thought, Mom and Pop would make it so unpleasant for him that it wouldn't make much difference. Grounded for a year, probably. Let them try to make that stick. They forced me into it anyway, he thought, by getting so uptight about my questions.

And if he succeeded, it would make it all worthwhile. If he found what he was looking for, he'd be able to carry on without difficulty. He'd have peace of mind—no matter what punishment he got. So he left by four-twenty, while Mrs. Sands was starting to fix dinner in the kitchen, and walked the mile to the market square.

There, facing him, was the Old Town Hall, built of light gray sandstone a hundred years before, with a historic plaque fastened to the front, to the right of the big doors.

The Enemy.

He went in and explored. First he examined the directory posted on the wall. Then, with a businesslike walk, he patrolled the building, as though he were an official and knew every foot of corridor.

The Birth and Death Registry was on the second floor at the intersection of two corridors, not far from the main staircase. It was neighbored on one side by the Land Surveyor's Office, and on the other by the Department of Parks. He looked inside: there was a long counter separating a small space for the public from the main office area, occupied by a half-dozen clerks sitting at desks. They looked to be mostly in their fifties, and mostly women. Covering the length of one wall was a series of metal cabinets with drawers.

Walking back to Mrs. Sands's house, he rehearsed the next morning's procedure.

He would enter the office, try to attract the attention of the kindliest-looking clerk, and ask if they could help him in his research....

Chris's father worked in an auto repair shop on the outskirts of Toronto. He was good at his trade, Chris's mother often said, but Chris thought when she said it that he would have no way of knowing; his father rarely took him to the shop and didn't seem to have a lot of time for him in general. He drank most weekends, and Chris had often found himself in the middle of nasty arguments between his parents. In return for his efforts, Chris had been at the receiving end of his father's anger. Yet the man had another side. Occasionally he'd show up at one of Chris's baseball or hockey games and cheer him on, and sometimes, when Chris least expected it, a sunny mood took over. When that happened the whole family seemed different: his dad, his mother, even Chris himself. It reminded him of happy times he called to mind from when he was very small. He didn't know why his father had changed. But he knew he had had a younger brother who died when he was still a baby, and he always thought that might have something to do with it.

His mother was a puzzle, too, but of a different kind. She always seemed to be doing something for somebody—taking soup to an invalid, reading to a blind woman, but Chris could never figure out what her own pleasures were unless it was just helping others that gave her joy. She went to church often, and seemed pleased when she could get her husband and son to go with her. Chris couldn't talk to her very easily, because she was rarely able to sympathize if he found fault with another person, whether it was another kid, a teacher, or anyone at all. It seemed as though Chris was always in the wrong, but when he told her that she said she just wanted to teach him to be humble and not criticize others. The particular situation he was in never really got her full attention so she could judge the question on its merits.

They were both good people in their way, Chris thought, but the thing that bothered him most was the way they'd never let him talk about his adoption.

He found out about it by accident. Obviously they would just as soon he'd stayed in the dark. One day when he was nine he'd been looking through an old family photo album. There were pictures of his parents and their families, then photographs of their courtship days, their wedding, and outings with their friends. Then Chris made his appearance, but as a toddler who was beginning to walk. There were no snapshots of Chris's mother holding him as an infant, or any pictures of him in a crib holding a rattle, or sitting up alone with a big grin. He'd wondered about the gap, and after going back to the album again and again he'd finally gotten up the courage to ask his mother about it.

Mom had looked startled, and told him his father's camera had been stolen just before Chris was born, and they'd been short of money so they couldn't buy a new one. But her manner had not reassured him; in fact, it had increased his uneasiness, so soon after he asked her whether there might be some other reason. "Like maybe I was very sick when I was a baby, or maybe I was even adopted!" Again she had evaded his questions. So he went to his father, and told him about the photographs and his unsatisfying talks with his mother. Pop had looked at him closely and asked, "So what do you think about it?"

"I wonder whether I'm adopted, like Charlie Cutler down the street." Charlie Cutler was a spoiled, overweight kid no one liked. He was also the only adopted person Chris knew. He hated to think of the possibility of being adopted if it meant being like Charlie in any way at all.

"Yes, you're adopted, Chris. You were eleven months old when you came to us. You're lucky to be here. Now don't talk about it anymore. It's bound to get Mother upset."

And Chris got no further explanation of why he had been adopted, or of anything relating to the event. He wasn't even sure, at that time of his life, just what adoption meant. He couldn't believe he was being shut off so abruptly from such a vital subject. But he was only nine years old, and there was nothing he could do.

So he kept it in, and wondered.

For four years he had followed his father's orders not to bring the subject up. He tried to kill the wonderings inside his head too, but he didn't succeed at that. When he was thirteen and beginning to feel his body change, he gained confidence. Some articles about adoption that he'd seen in the *Toronto Star* started him questioning his parents again.

He began talking to them one evening after supper. He asked cautiously, guiltily, as though he were doing a bad thing, because that was how they had made him feel, four years earlier. "Hey, I'd like to ask you something. You remember a few years ago I told you about not finding any baby pictures of myself in the album?"

His mother immediately got up to clear the dishes away, as though what he was saying weren't addressed to her.

He waited until she reappeared for more dishes and started again to talk to them both:

"Pop told me I was adopted, so I already know about that. But I was just wondering if you could tell me something about my parents."

He looked at his father sitting there in his blue work shirt, smoking a cigarette, his eyebrows knitted in concentration. Here it comes, thought Chris. "*We* are your parents, Christopher." It was said softly but with a tone of such finality that Chris knew they would never help him. His mother was busily going back and forth from the kitchen to the dining room as if nothing were happening.

So be it, thought Chris. He wasn't quite clear on what had just transpired, but he had an idea. It seemed as though his father had wanted to put him in the wrong for having used the word *parents*. As if Chris didn't know Mom and Pop were parents to him. To put him in the wrong, so he would shut up. But this time he didn't feel wrong, or guilty; instead he began to think that his parents were scared to face things. And maybe even a little dumb besides.

So he resolved to find out whatever he could on his own, without help from them.

And that was what had brought him to Kingston.

One day, not long after the useless talk with his parents, Chris was looking in his mother's file drawer for his high school course schedule.

Mom had a drawer in her kitchen where she kept all the family papers. Anything of importance that was printed or written on paper found its way there. Chris couldn't find his schedule on the top, so he rummaged through successively deeper layers: old receipted bills, canceled bank books, income tax forms. He was near the bottom of the pile when he came upon a small paper ripped from a spiral notebook, with a message that was puzzling in its simplicity:

>COMEAU
>Kingston
>5/1/66

It immediately caught Chris's attention; May 1 was his birthday.

He stood there wondering what it could mean, and in a moment the idea came to him that this was the name of his mother and the place of his birth.

Then, with some hesitation, he folded the slip of paper and put it in his wallet. If they're not going to help me, I'll just have to take charge of this, he thought. He had kept the slip with him ever since, like a talisman, and slowly formed the idea of tracking down this mysterious Miss or Mrs. Comeau.

Chris didn't know exactly what he would do if he found her. Ask her to take him home with her and save him from his wicked adoptive parents? Hardly. They weren't that bad. And doubtless this lady had a life of her own in which he wouldn't be especially welcome. After a lot of thought Chris had decided that what he really wanted was just to know a little about her, and if possible to learn something about his father, too. He didn't care all that much about actually meeting them, but since his mom and pop wouldn't tell him anything, he had no choice but to do some detective work. Which would surely mean talking to some people directly.

The biggest problem was how to get started.

Chris wasn't much of a reader. He was only an average student in school. But he was curious. He read the front page of the paper in addition to the sports section and the comics, and he often picked up news magazines like *Maclean's* or *Time*. He'd read a bit about adopted people and the searches they sometimes made. And he knew that there was something called a birth record which was the key to the search.

It contained the names of a person's original parents, and where they lived.

Before he went to sleep in Mrs. Sands's house that night, Chris pulled out his notebook. He flipped past the first few pages, where he'd written a few lines each day, and, choosing a clean page, he wrote:

> The dragon is a bunch of overweight ladies in a big room.
> The treasure is in metal file cabinets.
> Can Spider-Man trap the dragon in his web and flee with the treasure?
> Will the police, not knowing his true identity, bring him before the highest court in the land?
> Tune in tomorrow for the next episode of Spider-Man and the Dragon Ladies!

The next day was hazy and cool, with drizzles of rain. Chris had coffee and a doughnut in a small restaurant in the downtown section. He had, in fact, no idea what form these famous birth records took. Sitting with his second cup of coffee, he remembered reading about fat manila envelopes that unpleasant officials refused to hand over to angry, grown-up adoptees. He pictured himself asking, *Could I please see my fat, secret manila envelope?* He chuckled in spite of himself. Then he remembered another thought he'd had. What if there were a ledger in which all births were recorded for each day, consecutively, over the years? Then it was logical—if the slip of paper he'd discovered meant what he thought it did—that he would find his mother's name listed under the date of his birth, perhaps with other information that could help him find her. This, at least, was the line of thinking that he'd been following when he prepared for the visit he was about to make.

But it all depended on whether or not he was allowed to see the ledger.

If, if, and if. His search depended on so many *ifs* that he was suddenly discouraged, sitting there in the restaurant. He looked around him, noticed the dingy wallpaper and the hairy mole on the middle-aged waitress's cheek, and felt tired, shabby, sneaky and alone.

It was only nine-ten in the morning.

Entering the Town Hall, Chris went straight to the birth records office. He had on his windbreaker with deep pockets; it suited the weather that day, but, more important, it was part of Chris's plan. He had thought that if he ever did get his hands on a folder that was specifically about him, and if the officials were reluctant to let him see the whole thing, an opportunity might arise to simply make off with it by sticking it in his capacious pocket when no one was looking, running out of the building, and going in whatever direction gave the best escape.

Room 231 was quietly busy when Chris entered. He surveyed the personnel in the office: three middle-aged fat ladies (MFL's, as Chris and his friends used to refer to some of the teachers in the high school) and a short man with glasses who looked mousy. He couldn't tell who was in charge. One of the women had been joking with the man when Chris came in, and because her face looked pretty human when she smiled, he decided to start with her. He stationed himself at the counter opposite her desk, and she looked up pleasantly.

"What can I do for you, son?"

"I was hoping I could have a look at the birth register."

The woman looked puzzled. "I'm doing a demographic project for my school. It's to determine birth rates in different towns in southern Ontario and to see if I can relate them to chemical changes in the environment."

"Well, I don't know, young man. Where do you go to school?"

"Perkins Secondary School in Toronto. It's for my biology course. Extra credit. I've already been in Oshawa, Trenton, and Belleville, and I'm going to Brockville last. A heck of a way to spend a summer vacation!" And he flashed her a grin. He'd been reasonably sure that if he mentioned adoption, all would be lost.

"We don't usually allow anyone to examine the records. I'm afraid you'll have to speak to the supervisor about this. In a few moments, the supervisor approached Chris with a thin, businesslike smile. "I'm Mrs. Gray. What can I do for you? Mrs. O'Neill tells me you have some sort of a school project?"

Chris knew this was the encounter that could make or break his effort. He debated whether or not to give his real name. If he did, and the woman decided to check on him, he was dead. But if he didn't, he couldn't use the I.D. cards he had—or the special letter he had composed for this occasion. He decided to risk it and try to charm the ladies so they wouldn't feel a need to check up.

He told his story in more detail to Mrs. Gray, and showed her the letter, typed on a piece of stationery he had taken from the office at school.

> To whom it may concern:
>
> This will introduce Christopher Miller, a tenth grade student in our school. He is engaged in a research project which tries to relate fluctuations in birth rate in various towns to the presence of noxious chemicals introduced to the environment within the last fifteen years. To this end

we would very much appreciate your giving him access to the birth records of your town and the surrounding townships, for the first six months of the years 1966 and 1981. Chris is competing for the National High School Science Award and we have hopes he will make a genuine contribution to ecology.

>Sincerely yours,
>Dennis Roach, Headmaster
>Henry Levy, Chairman of the Science Department

Chris had taken infinite pains with this letter, since writing (or spelling, for that matter) was not his strong point. He'd torn up seven prior versions. Naturally, the whole idea was invented, and the signatures were forged. He was especially proud of his fancy language: "engaged in," "to this end," "we have hopes." He had spent several hours looking through a textbook of business correspondence to pick up some high-toned phrases.

Mrs. Gray smiled after reading the letter and said, "I admire your industry, Chris. Can you show me any other identification?"

Chris pulled out his wallet and showed his Scout membership card, his student I.D. with a photograph, and the card that showed he belonged to a Presbyterian youth group.

To his amazement the woman seemed convinced. "I can't see where it would do any harm to let you look through the ledgers. Here, come through this gate and use one of the desks; Miss Kelleher won't be in today." And she brought out two large books labeled *Births, 1966* and *Births, 1981*. Chris couldn't believe his good fortune as he sat like an official at an expensive aluminum desk, on a swivelling office chair, and the clerks left him to his business.

He'd brought a pad of lined paper. He wrote across the top of the front sheet, in capitals, the names of the towns and townships in the Kingston area, and borrowed a straightedge from the desktop to make it look orderly....

Half an hour and many pencil-marks later, Chris arrived at May 1, 1966. He'd deliberately resisted the temptation to jump right to the date, mainly for fear that what he was looking for wouldn't be there. He didn't want his bubble to burst so suddenly. While trying to make a tally of the births in each town for each month of the year, he'd been familiarizing himself with the pages of the register. The entries were made by date; each day would have a clump of entries under it. Some had as many as ten, while other dates were omitted, presumably because no births had occurred on those days. Most entries started with a last name and a man and woman's first name; then there was a space for their address, their religion, the child's place of birth, boy or girl, the attending physician's name, and comments. Place of birth was generally given as KGH—this must mean Kingston General Hospital—St. Luke's, or other names of hospitals. About 5 percent were listed as HD, which Chris thought must mean home delivery.

And occasionally he ran across an entry which gave only a woman's last and first name, with the notation under comments, "Placed for adoption."

Chris had arrived at May 1. The fourth entry under that date read as follows:

COMEAU, Nancy, 18 Sheffield Street, Elgin.
Catholic. KGH. Boy. Dr. Stokes.
Placed for adoption.

Chris was breathing hard and he felt his heart pounding

in his chest. He didn't know how he was going to sit for another hour or so making marks on paper when the key to his past was staring him in the face. But he knew he had no choice; if he didn't behave as the clerks expected him to, they would smell a rat. And they knew who he was and where he came from.

He felt no need for a fat folder. *Nancy Comeau, 18 Sheffield Street, Elgin* was enough for him. His task completed by a quarter to eleven, he thanked the ladies with a broad grin and some graceful words, and escaped. He ran down the granite staircase. Seeing the sun break through the overcast sky, he began singing the Beatles' "Here Comes the Sun" at full voice, and passers-by turned and stared.

He'd never heard of Elgin. When he asked the manager of a Fina station where it was, he pronounced it with a soft *g,* like the name of the wristwatch, and the man corrected him. "Elgin, like *begin.* It's a little crossroads up in the Rideau Lakes." He gave him a road map and pointed out the small dot that indicated the village.

How old would my mother be now? Chris wondered. Thirty? Forty? Would she still be in that crossroads in the Rideau Lakes? And after a while, another thought peeped out of its hole like a mouse afraid of a cat: Would she still remember me?

Elgin, with all its remoteness, turned out to be less than thirty miles from Kingston. Chris had found a bus that took him as far as Seeleys Bay, and he thumbed the remaining few miles. The man in the Fina station hadn't been exaggerating about its small size; Chris judged there could scarcely be more than a hundred houses in the village. Luckily, a few of them rented rooms; this was, after all, still fishing country. He went into the general store and invested in a cheap spin-cast rod and reel and a few hooks and bobbers to look more convincing. As it turned out, the store owners had a room to rent on the second floor, right above the store. The room had an old brass four-poster bed, and Chris was comfortably installed on the same day he had left Kingston.

He had been gone ten days. He wondered what his parents were thinking, and he felt a twinge of sadness that his flight had been so successful. A police badge flashed at him would have messed up his plans, but it would have shown him how worried they were. As it was, he could only guess.

The local phone directory covered seventeen towns. There were two "Comeau" listings in Elgin, and both of them were on Sheffield Street. Chris found the street about two minutes' walk from the general store. It was almost a country lane. He walked along it whistling.

Number 18 was the largest house on the street, which wasn't saying much. It was a white frame two-story dwelling with children's toys strewn on the front lawn, and clothes on a clothesline out back. A small placard in a front window advertised FRESH BAKED BREAD, and Chris could smell it baking. And stuck in the ground next to the path to the back door was another sign: WORMS.

I wonder which way it'll turn out, thought Chris. Bread, or worms.

Walking around, thinking about what to do next, he learned where the kids hung out. Close to the general store someone had set up a basketball hoop. Half a dozen boys from twelve to eighteen hung out there, shooting baskets. Without ceremony Chris was invited to join the boys on the court.

"Hey, want to play two on two?"

That was his introduction to Elgin society.

For three days he did little but fish and play basketball. When anyone showed curiosity about Chris he explained that he was visiting an uncle who lived a couple of miles out of town. His uncle's wife didn't want him around the house all day, so he was hanging around the village a lot.

He waited for an opening to ask questions.

On the third day Art, one of the older boys, mentioned Jim Comeau. He was talking about some local farmers.

Chris felt his skin prickle. He interrupted, "I've heard that name before. I think I heard my uncle say he was a friend of his. Where does he live?"

"Comeau? His farm's out on Route 15, south of here, but he has another house in town. I think his daughter lives there with her family, and they've an old aunt or something on the same street. I don't know them real well."

Chris called out, "See you. I just remembered something." He was gone in a second, blazing down the street with no destination, his mind in a whirl.

He ran five miles, slow and easy, just to work up a sweat and not have to think. Then he spent the rest of the day lying on his bed, unable to keep the thoughts away any longer. Why had he gone on this stupid quest anyhow? And what on earth did he hope to gain from it?

His flesh prickled again, and for a second he caught himself wishing he had his old teddy bear with him to keep him company. He realized he was afraid.

That night Chris had another dream. In this one he entered a large farm kitchen with the fragrance of newly baked bread; a middle-aged woman with full breasts and a youthful face smiled at him and kissed him on the cheek; her husband shook his hand warmly and clapped him on the back. *We're proud of you,* they said, and gave him bread and jam to eat.

When he awoke his arms and legs were leaden with fatigue. His stomach was in knots; he felt warm, his head ached, and he was sure he was seriously ill. He asked to borrow his landlady's thermometer, but it showed no fever. He forced down two aspirins and some orange juice, then went to sit on the bank of the stream. After ten minutes he couldn't delay any longer. It was nine in the morning on the tenth of August, and he'd been a runaway for two weeks. God knew how many laws and ordinances he had broken in that time, and what he was about to do might not be against the law but it terrified him. He had to finish and get back to being a boy again.

On Sheffield Street he looked from a distance at number 18. All his symptoms returned when he saw the house. There was no car there; Chris hoped that meant her husband had gone to work. Trying to put on a cheerful face, he went up to the screen door and knocked. Presently a slim, pretty woman in her early thirties with long blond hair came to greet him. She had a cigarette in her hand, and a small child clothed only in a diaper came toddling after her.

"I wonder if I could buy a loaf of bread?"

"Sure thing. Just baked this morning."

Her voice was deeper than he'd expected, and he noticed lines on her face. She took a loaf and wrapped it in a plastic bag. "That'll be fifty cents."

Standing on her porch, he handed over the money, but didn't take the bread. "Say, would you by any chance be Jim Comeau's daughter?"

"Yes, my name's Nancy Hanlon. You know my dad?" She sounded tired, but in her raspy voice there was a chipper quality that he liked.

"Well, I came over from Toronto with my father to do some fishing, and he said he had an old war buddy named Jim Comeau that lived around here. And when he asked about him, someone in town said his daughter lived here. Just thought I'd ask."

She looked at him carefully for the first time. He felt her eyes on his hair, his face, measuring the breadth of his shoulders. She put down his bread on the folding card table that served as her bakery counter and fell backward a step.

"Is anything wrong? Can I help?"

"There's something strange here. You look like . . . you look like someone I used to know. What did you say your name was?"

"Miller, Chris Miller."

"I never heard Dad talk about anyone named Miller. Look, what is this anyway?" Her eyes were hostile. The child began to cry.

Chris had been standing there with years of stored-up feelings churning inside him, and he couldn't keep them in any more. With a choked voice he said, "I was born on May 1, 1966."

The woman sat down heavily in a wicker chair. She began to cry, at first quietly, and then in deep sobs. Chris didn't know what to do. He began to walk toward her chair, but she looked up at him with such fear in her eyes that Chris began to feel like a criminal. "Look, I just wanted to meet you. I didn't want to cause any trouble. If this is a bad time, maybe I could come back tomorrow."

"No . . . Tell me your name again."

"Chris."

"No, Chris. That sounds so funny. I thought you would be Lewis, but things didn't work out." And she began crying again, and Chris could see that her nose needed blowing, so without thinking he handed her his clean pocket handkerchief. She accepted it, and took the still-crying child on her lap and rocked it gently, and Chris stood there with tears running down his own cheeks. She looked at him and handed back his handkerchief. There was a silence.

"Hey, are you all right? I'm sorry, I'm really sorry. I just had to see what you looked like. And I thought maybe you could tell me something about . . . about him."

"Sam doesn't know. That's my husband. These kids' Dad." And she made a wide gesture that included her baby, the bicycles and toys on the lawn, and the main part of the house from which Chris had been vaguely aware of voices. "He doesn't know, do you understand?" There was an intensity in her voice that was almost hatred. Chris wished he were in some remote part of China.

"I'm sorry." And with an intensity of his own he added, "I'm sorry, Mrs. Hanlon." The woman looked up in surprise.

"Oh, my God, my God. 'Mrs. Hanlon,' you said. Oh, my God. I cried so much over you, I thought there were no tears left." The tears came again as she stood up slowly, falteringly, holding the child by the hand as she put it gently on the ground. She came hesitantly to Chris, put her arms around him, and kissed him on the cheek. He hugged her cautiously, fearfully. He felt the dampness of her tears. "I hoped you wouldn't come, and I hoped you would. You look just like him. Here, come into the house. You can't stay long. The neighbors will talk, and Sam comes home for lunch at noon."

Chris met her older children, six and nine years old. She told them he was a cousin from Vancouver that she hadn't seen for years. Chris felt cheated at this deception though he knew she had no choice. She sent them out to play.

"What was he like? Where is he?"

"A big fellow, like you. He worked in construction. A good guy, but he was like a kid. When he found out you were coming along he got scared off. I would have married him, too. I loved the guy. I hear he's over in Deseronto now with a family of his own. I think about him a lot. But Sam doesn't know. Sam's a good man, but I don't know what he'd do if he found out. Here, have a cup of coffee. Lord, you're a handsome boy. By now you must be . . ."

"Fifteen."

"Fifteen. How well I know. . . . To look at you, I would-'ve said sixteen at least. Tell me about yourself."

Chris breathed a prayer of thanks that they had got past the tense scene on the porch. "First tell me about you."

"I'm fine. Nobody brings up my past that knows it. We don't live a fancy life up here, you know. Sam works as an attendant at the mental hospital, and I keep the books for Thompson's electronics business. I have a good family, and I sing a lot and teach the piano—music keeps the soul alive, they say."

Chris noticed for the first time an upright piano in the corner; otherwise the room was furnished with nothing but a plain table covered with an oilcloth, chairs that didn't match, and a television set. It was a combination kitchen, dining room, and living room.

"I'm glad . . . I'm glad. We live in Toronto, me and my mom and pop. They had another kid that died when I was small. We're not rich either."

"What are they like, your mom and pop? Do they treat you nice?"

How could he condense fifteen years of living? What good would it do to talk about his father's drinking, or his mother's dull existence? "They're pretty regular people. Brought me up O.K."

"That's good. . . . Do you study hard in school? Do you get good grades? That's important, you know."

Chris's eyes began to fill. He'd never met this woman until fifteen minutes ago, and she was expressing concern over his education. Like a mother. He burst into sobs he couldn't control. Nancy Hanlon came over, picked up her littlest one in her left arm, and with the other cradled Chris's head against her body. Chris let himself stay there for a moment. But the feelings of longing and confusion he had were too much. He felt like a little boy, and a grown man, and a lost soul, all at the same time. He stood up.

"I have to go now. Good to see you. I'll write sometime." He wiped his eyes with his forearm; still half-blinded by tears, he blundered out of the room, across the porch, and out the screen door.

She came after him quickly, bewildered, and called plaintively, "His name's Charlie Hughes!" And after a moment, "Hey, you forgot your bread! Chris, you forgot your bread!"

But Chris was out of sight.

Nancy Hanlon looked at the two quarters on the table, and the wrapped up loaf of bread, and her shoulders shook with renewed sobbing. Her baby came over and peered seriously into her eyes, and the two older ones came out from the back of the house and looked at each other.

"Come on, Ma," the older one said. "He's just a cousin."

COMMENTARY
ADOPTION
SEARCHING
RELATIONSHIPS
LAWS

Chris is a stubborn kid. He goes after what he wants. He finds his birth mother after some clever detective work and much persistence. But it costs him something: he has to lie a lot, and at the end he's exhausted. Did he find what he was after? And what will he do with it now?

Nobody knows for certain how many adopted people want to do what Chris did and how many are content to live their lives without searching. And nobody knows whether most of the ones who search have parents like Chris's, who don't approve of their son's or daughter's curiosity about biological heritage.

What is a *biological heritage*? The knowledge of what your birth parents looked and sounded like, where their families came from, what they did for a living, what they liked to eat, what jokes they laughed at, and a thousand other things.

And why is your biological heritage important if you have a mother and father who care for you and provide for your needs? Do you need to know about your birth parents? Is it enough to know about them, or should you have the right to meet them? If so, at what age? These are big questions today. And they're not just questions that people wonder about privately. The opening of birth records to adoptees (usually at age eighteen) is a political issue now. Bills are introduced in state legislatures every year to help adoptees locate their birth parents, and usually these bills are defeated. Why is there such a battle about this, and why hasn't our society found some way to help people be more comfortable about adoption?

And since we've gone this deep, what is adoption, anyway? Where does it fit in, in our country, and in our towns and cities, in our churches and clubs and schools and families?

There are people who look down at the floor when they say, "I was adopted." There are others who are quite comfortable in stating this fact about themselves. But for some reason, a lot of adopted people seem to feel that being adopted means there's something the matter with them. They keep coming back to an old idea they had when they were six or eight or ten: "I must have been bad, or they would have kept me."

Throughout human history, babies have been born to mothers and fathers who sometimes couldn't take good care of them. These adults may have been sick, physically or emotionally, or they may have been too young or too poor to take on the big responsibility of a child.

In some places children born to very young parents could stay in the family, because it was common for adolescents to be sexually active and common for their parents to take on the care of children born to their teenage sons or daughters. Traditionally this has been a common situation among only some groups in our own country. It is increasingly common now, though, for young women to keep their infants.

But when circumstances don't allow this kind of solution to the problem, a child needs substitute parents. In some countries or tribes, the child went to relatives to be raised. (These children grew up knowing their original parents and having some relationship with them.) In others, the birth parents arranged for the baby to be raised by nonrelated people who were more wealthy than they, or who could later teach the child a trade that would support him or her through adult life. (These children usually maintained some kind of connection with their birth parents, but it was rather distant—perhaps a visit or two each year.)

Gradually, over the last hundred and fifty years, adoption in America and Europe evolved from a kind of long-term foster care arrangement (in which children usually grew up very self-conscious about their origins outside the family, and were often reminded of them) into the present system. Nowadays adopted children have all the legal rights and privileges of "home-made" ones, and parents are encouraged to think of them as their own kids in every way.

In the twentieth century the idea became accepted that it was not important for babies placed with adoptive families to know their original parents—or even to know *about* them. Social workers, doctors, and lawyers all agreed that what was important was the child's relationship with the adoptive parents. (At that time the vast majority of adoptions involved infants or children so young that they could remember very little about their original caretakers, so it is perhaps understandable why people might have thought that, from the child's point of view, there was really no past that could be important to the child.) Frequently they were lied to ("Your parents were both killed in an auto accident"), or not even told that they had been adopted at all.

When they knew of it and showed curiosity about their birth parents, a common idea, twenty or thirty years ago, was that this showed "poor adjustment." People thought that since there had never been a relationship, the kid who kept thinking about these "other parents" must be living in a dream world. The child was thought to be neurotic, or else people said that the relationships within the adoptive home must be troubled.

Today most professional people associated with adoption don't think this way. They are beginning to recognize that though *some* adoptees' strong interest in their roots may be related to troubles within the adoptive family, it is more often not a question of family problems. Many adoptees have a perfectly normal interest in where they came from, genetically speaking, and in the circumstances of their birth parents' lives and the reasons they were placed for adoption.

This gets us back to where we were at the beginning of this commentary. It might be useful to think about Chris and his adoptive family, how he arrived at the decision to search, and what he got—and didn't get—from the experience.

He grew up in a family that probably started out pretty average in most ways. But by the time we learn about them, the warts on his parents are pretty obvious. His father drinks too much, his mother is a boring do-gooder, and neither of them is much good at talking about feelings. Probably losing their first child left them with emotional scars. Or maybe they would have wound up like this anyway—people who just aren't much fun, like Dorothy's aunt and uncle in *The Wizard of Oz*. But from Chris's point of view, the worst thing about his parents is that they couldn't be straight with him about his adoption.

Chris's adoptive parents, the Millers, are an example of what the sociologist David Kirk has called "denial-of-difference families." That is, they don't want to think that adopting a child is any different from having one born to them. They hold this attitude so strongly that they don't even tell Chris he's adopted, and when he finds out by accident (as many kids do who aren't told before they're seven or eight), they can't deal with it. One interesting possibility is that keeping this secret, and refusing to face facts once the secret is out, is a big part of what wears these people out.

They seem to think that if they act as though the fact of adoption weren't there, neither they nor Chris will ever have to think about it.

If they had let themselves face the fact that Chris wasn't born to them, and had told him about it little by little from the time he was four or five or six, they would have felt sad at times, and Chris would have felt even sadder. But probably they would have been able to help each other with their sadness, and then would have moved on to live their lives more comfortably.

Even then, Chris might have decided he wanted to search—but it probably would have been later, maybe when he was in his twenties, when he felt more ready and less driven. By then he wouldn't have felt so troubled about where his loyalties lay, or so alone in his search.

If he *didn't* decide to search, that would have been normal, too. Some people decide that it simply isn't worth the hassle, and though they are sometimes troubled by wondering about what might have been, isn't that true of everybody in one way or another? A phrase sometimes used for this kind of solution to a conflict is "cutting your losses and moving on."

Chris and his birth mother have a blood tie. Does that mean they have a relationship? The question is tricky. It's a little like asking whether a drinking glass is a container or not. You might say, "Of course it's a container, just like a soda can or a gallon jug." But someone else who took longer to think about it might say, "It depends on circumstances. If there's water or juice or milk in it, then it's *acting* as a container. Otherwise it just has the *potential* to be one."

That's one way to look at the question of a relationship between Chris Miller and Nancy Hanlon. Then we might conclude, "A relationship is a connection between two people that's alive and has meaning for both of them." Then in the story, at the beginning, there is no relationship. What there is, instead, is:

1. The blood tie between Chris and his birth mother;
2. Chris's longing to know about her; and
3. Nancy Hanlon's wonderings over the years about the child she gave birth to.

These things don't add up to a relationship. It's like the empty glass. But at the end, things are a bit different. By taking matters into his own hands, Chris has brought about a situation in which the two of them are truly connected, at least for a few moments. We would have to say that there, on the porch, they were related to each other.

Whether this fragile relationship survives, in the form of continuing contacts, depends on whether they both want it to, and whether they are able to bring it off. For some adoptees and birth parents, even a moment of relationship is a lot better than none at all.

Part of the difficulty of all this is that laws and customs are mostly against these relationships forming or continuing. As already mentioned, there is a push for new laws to allow adoptees access to their birth records at age eighteen. At the present time, only four states in the United States have open records: Alabama, Alaska, Kansas, and Pennsylvania. Another five states have mutual consent laws, by which an adoptee and a birth parent may learn each other's identity only if both have already signed a statement that they are willing. (And to illustrate how things change, Massachusetts, the state where this is being written, was an open record state ten years ago until a law reversed that situation!)

You might wonder why birth parents might not be willing to be contacted. Why would open records not be a mutual, taken-for-granted thing? (And, for that matter—though this is too big a question to look at in this commentary—why wait until age eighteen to open records?) Why all this secrecy, anyway?

Some adoption social workers are concerned that if birth mothers are not guaranteed secrecy, they will choose not to give birth to their infants. They mention that far fewer babies are available for adoption now than fifteen years ago. The concern about whether a pregnancy is carried to term might be valid in the case of some birth mothers, but the present scarce supply of healthy infants for adoption has other causes as well as the increased availability of abortion. Contraception (including the pill) was not as available fifteen years ago, especially for teenagers. What's more, the possibility of unmarried women keeping their baby without "losing face," is much more likely. What cannot be denied, though, is that birth parents—especially mothers—are often in a vulnerable situation.

If a woman is unmarried and hopes to marry someday, she may fear what a man's reaction would be if he learned that she had had a child. If she enters into marriage with this fear, still keeping it secret from her husband, it becomes harder and harder to raise the subject as the months and years pass. We may believe that keeping secrets, in general, is not such a good thing to do; but if a woman has begun with a secret from her husband and family, she may be terrified that her life would fall apart if they learned of it. So the secret continues, and the woman wants to be protected from her past, though she may yearn secretly for knowledge of the child she gave up so long ago.

Many adoptive parents, too, are interested in keeping the barriers up. They are afraid that a birth parent might approach their child and confuse him or her. And they are concerned that their teenager might be lost to them if a birth parent appeared and seemed to offer instant understanding at a time when the adolescent was still trying to work things out with the adoptive parents. It's unlikely that this latter fear has much foundation, but, certainly, the younger a kid is, the more probable it is that the child would be confused if Original Mother or Father suddenly appeared.

Some adoptive parents are also afraid that their kids will do what Chris did, or something like it, and that this too would lead to their losing a son or daughter. (And if records were available, they fear it would be even easier for this to happen.) Many feel so strongly about this that they contribute time and money to defeat legislative bills for open records.

On the other side, many adoptees and birth parents, as well as some adoptive parents, are trying to open things up so that people won't have to sneak around and feel guilty in order to learn about their roots.

Many organizations now exist for adoptees, adoptive

parents, and birth parents to help them pursue their goals. There are, in addition, a number of "reunion registries" which are sometimes able to mediate the coming together of an adoptee and a birth parent. Since the organizations are so numerous I will mention only one of them here: the American Adoption Congress, Box 23641 L'Enfant Plaza, Washington, D.C. 20024, which is a good source of information for anyone in the United States.

Readers interested in learning more about the history of adoption may want to read *So You're Adopted,* by Fred Powledge. Older teenagers may be interested in *The Politics of Adoption,* by Mary Kathleen Benet, and *The Adoption Triangle,* by Arthur D. Sorosky, Annette Baran, and Reuben Pannor (see the reading list at the end of the book).

JOANNA

1720 Claremont Avenue
Chicago, Illinois
January 3, 1980

Dear Miss Briggs,

    It's been some time since we've seen each other; I think the last time was at that meeting in Denver a few years back. I hope you are in good health. I am writing about Joanna, the little girl whose foster care you supervised fourteen years ago. As you may recall, I took over the case when you were made director of the agency, just prior to her adoptive placement. I know that, with your famous memory for clients, you will quickly call Joanna to mind.

    Joanna has made a request which I will relay to you at the end of this very large letter; but I hope you will proceed in order through it, as you may get some pleasure from the way it unfolds. As you will have noticed, I enclose a number of letters from Joanna before my own final sheet; I have her permission and encouragement to show them to you.

As you remember, Joanna and her younger brother Kevin came into care following a neglect report. The two children, then aged six and three, were living with their mother Louise, who had many bouts of drinking and mental illness. They were dirty and poorly clothed. The little girl had become a sort of mother to her own mother, but was often beaten by her, with fervent apologies afterward. When placed with the Simmons family she was first thought by the foster mother to be retarded because she always hesitated before answering a question; I recall you pointed out to Mrs. Simmons that the child was merely being cautious, given her past experience. She did some stealing from the Simmonses, too, and that persisted, but we felt it would subside in a good adoptive home. You will remember that such a home was found two years after the foster placement.

I remained in touch with Joanna after her move, since both she and I derived pleasure from the contact, and her adoptive parents didn't mind. When she was twelve, my husband Richard got his teaching job in Chicago. After the wonderful party you all gave for me, we packed up our things and took the trek northward; I then began to work in my present agency. Joanna and I would still write to one another once a year or so, and I got a picture of her development as it progressed.

September 13, 1966

Dear Miss French,

Thank you for the book. I loked at it. It has nice pitures. But I wish you sent me candy insted. I had my 8th brithday here with my knew Mom and Dad. They had a cake but I had no frends here Ive only been here 2 weeks.

I crid myself to sleep last night I got a letter from Lou in the hospitel. Im puting it in here becase if I keep it I dont know what to do with it itmakes me sad. I get nasty a lot. Pleas write

Joanna

Dear Jo

I hope your happy now. They decided to take you away from me. So I guess your on your own. I was going to take you from the foster home when I got out of here. But the big shots in the state said I shouldn't have you. So youll go to another family. When your bigger youl know they shouldent do this to me. Nobody ever helped me exept Jesus and he dident help much.

I love you always,
Your mother, Lou

September 20, 1967

Dear Miss French,

I dont see you often like I used to. Since I'm with my new dad and mom I guess I dont need to see you so much but I miss you and my old worker Miss Brigs. I was glad you came to my party I hope you liket my Home and my friends. I always write Thank You letters my mommy Lou said always to do that so I'm writeing even thogh I just saw you.

I really liked the big Whitmans sampler box you now I like Chocolate. I was terrible last year writing you should have sent candy. Lou always said be glad for what you got. I got another letter from her but I didnt cry as much.

Can you help me find out about Kevin I really want to see him. Is he still with Mrs. Simmons? Are you still his worker?

I'm not stealing as much but I tok my older sister Julie's braclet last week and got in trouble.

Love,
Joanna

June 14, 1968

Dear Mrs. Finney,

It sounds very strang to write Mrs. Finney when I always called you Miss French. I am writing because you got married. I don't have much money for a marrage present as I have to pay back some money because I took some. So I wrote a poem for your marrage instead.

I have known you very long.
You have helped me know right from wrong.
You are pretty as a butterfly
And I hope you do not sigh.
I hope your husband is a fine man
Tall and handsome with a tan.
I hope that I can be like you
And do nice things for people too.

I think the third and forth line are a bit arkward but I did my best. I can't say what I feel in the letter just in the poem.

Love,
Joanna

September 18, 1968

Dear Mrs. Finney,

It's so long since I've seen you. I'm writing on my new stationery with my initials. Mom said she'd get me something special if I did better for a few months, and I did, and this is it. Isn't it neat?

I'm ten years old now. Dad said that I'm in the double digits. I guess he means I'll never be a little kid again.

Thanks a lot for the beautiful earrings. I realy feel like a big shot now! I want to get my ears peirced but Mom says I'm too young. If I ever do I'll have the earrings convurted.

I'm doing better in school this year. I started in the fifth grade and I have a 90 and a 95 on quizzes so far. My teacher said she thougt I was bright. I never thougt of that. I'm in Brownies too. My best friend Jennifer is in my class and in my Brownie troop too. She has blond hair, not like my black hair, I wish mine was like hers.

My parents took me to see Kevin last month. He's still in the same foster home with Mrs. Simmons. It was good to see Mom and Dad Simmons again and it was great to see Kevin. He still has that cute smile and the dimple in his chin and he remembered a joke I told him a long time ago. I get to see him a couple times a year. It's not enough. Why do they say he's not adoptable? He can even play baseball. Please, are you still working with Kevin? Maybe you can help.

Love,
Joanna

September 14, 1969

Dear Mrs. Finney,

I have the most wonderful news. Kevin is going to come live with us and be adopted like me! Mom told me last month but I waited till now to tell you because I always write to you in September.

I guess Mom and Dad were thinking about adopting Kevin for a long time but didn't want to tell me because I might be disappointed if it didn't work out. Maybe you knew about it too. I guess you must have. The state wouldn't let him be adopted because he had a heart murmer and was hyper-active (what does *that* mean?) but mainly because our first mother kept hoping she could take him, but she kept on not being able to and she finally said O.K.

We all went to the Simmonses' house to tell Kevin—Mom, Dad, Julie and I. Kevin is 8 now and really cute. He couldn't believe it, he was so happy but he was sad too and so were the Simmonses even though they have 2 kids of their own and 2 other foster kids.

I love the diary you sent me. I started writing in it as soon as I opened it on my birthday and I'll try to write in it every day. I'm glad you keep in touch with me. I'm really happy about Kevin and I bet you are, too.

Love,
Joanna

September 20, 1970

Dear Mrs. Finney,

It's too bad you have to move away from Kansas City. You've been part of my life for so long that I can't picture not having you around, even though I've only seen you once or twice a year lately. But I'm glad your husband got such a good job teaching college. He sounds important, and I bet he's handsome too.

Speaking of that I have a "boyfriend." His name is Danny, and he has blond hair and he's one of the best students in school. I say "boyfriend" with quoteation marks because I don't know if he likes me.

Kevin had a hard time for a while, really he still is. He's been here 8 months now. He looks out the window and won't talk for days, and he breaks things. I didn't realize till now what I must have been like the first few years. I haven't stolen anything for a long time now, and I can talk to Mom about most things, and Dad about the rest. I never used to talk to them; I think I wanted to make them guess what I was thinking.

Mom has been talking to me about growing up. She says I'm going to be a woman soon. I can't decide if I think it's funny or scary.

Please don't stop writing just because you're far away. I think I'll stop by the agency next week to say goodbye. And maybe I'll come to see you in Chicago some day.

Love,
Joanna

P. S. I almost forgot to thank you for the toilet water. I love lily of the valley. My mother Lou used to have the same kind (did you know that?) and when I smelled it I couldn't help it, I started crying. I don't know where she is now. I'll wear it and think of her and you.

J.

September 25, 1971

Dear Mrs. Finney,

What great news! I think being pregnant is terrific. It's something I've devoted some thought to. (Do not fear, I have excellent judgment.) Do you want a girl or a boy? I'll bet your husband wants a boy and you want a girl.

I'm in eighth grade now, one of the big shots! I play flute in the orchestra, and I have mostly A's in school. I definitely want to go to college, but I'm not sure what I want to do after that. I'm thinking about being a lawyer like Dad.

You sent me a book again. I remember the last time you did that, and what I said. But this time I was ready. I love reading, and I can't eat much candy anyway because I'm watching my weight! I loved Willa Cather's *My Antonia*, and have already read it twice! It gave me a new idea about what women have contributed to this country. It was a wonderful gift for my thirteenth birthday.

Speaking of women, last year I told you Mom said I was going to be one soon. Well, now I am.

Sincerely yours,
Joanna

September 16, 1972

Dear Mrs. Finney,

Well, I'm in high school now, and Kevin is in 6th grade. Time marches on! I think about you and sometimes I want to forget you, because you come from a part of my life that I don't like to think about much anymore. I keep on growing up, and doing more things (I went out West this summer with my family and learned to ride a horse!), and I think about what a brat I was and how sad I was and it seems like two different me's.

Kevin is coming around. He took longer than I did. But now he plays in the band, and gets O.K. grades, and plays baseball and soccer, and has lots of friends. Sometimes he still gives Mom and Dad a hard time when he's tired or upset about something, or when he's pushed with some kind of a job to do, and he says, "You're not my real parents. You can't tell me what to do." Usually what happens then is that people tell him to cut the c——, and he does. But sometimes he cries, or they cry, or I cry, or we all cry. Lou's ghost is floating in the air when that happens. I think it's worse not knowing where she is and whether she's dead or alive. The last I heard was almost a year ago; she called on the phone and sounded really drunk, and promised to take Kevin and me to Disney World if we would meet her in Mobile, Alabama, the next day. Kev really wanted to go, and he cried a lot that night. I did, too, a little. Mom and Dad were pretty good about it; they never really said no, and Kevin finally realized himself that the chances she would be there if we went to meet her were pretty slim. I wish we could do something for her, but I still hate her, too—mostly for making Kevin cry that night, and all the other promises she made that she didn't keep. Mom says it's not our job to help her, and we couldn't do it anyway if we tried.

This letter is getting long. Thanks a lot for the Picasso reproduction. I've learned a little about him and I really like his blue period; I actually knew that picture with the clown family on the beach already, and it was a favorite of mine. I have it in a frame on my wall, and those beautiful lonely performers make me think of lots of different things.

I don't know how to sign anymore, so I'm just

Joanna

P.S. I loved the Polaroid picture of you and the baby. He's adorable! And you look the same as always.

November 1, 1973

Dear Mrs. Finney,

I think you're right about presents. I am, as you say, not a kid anymore, and to get a birthday letter from you is enough of a present when I'm fifteen and have so many people in my life right here in K.C. who care for me. Besides, you must have spent a small fortune on me by now. My delay in answering your nice letter is not because of your new policy about birthday presents.

When I wrote you a year ago I mentioned something about Lou's ghost. I must have been having a premonition, because right around my birthday Kevin and I got word that she was in a hospital in Joplin on the critical list. We all drove over to see her—my parents had never met her, but they knew what it meant to Kev and me. (You should see him; he's a real hunk now, and doing well in school.)

Anyhow, we got there and she was in the last stages of liver failure and died within a day without recognizing us. We got a motel room, but we only had to stay two nights—one while she finished dying, and another one while we made the funeral arrangements. There was no one else to do it. Kevin and I were so sad, but Mom and Dad were wonderful; they told us they loved Lou for having raised us as long as she did, and they made all the phone calls and arrangements and paid for the funeral.

It was very hard for me, the whole thing: seeing her there, looking so terrible, and thinking what she had done to herself all those years, and watching the dirt fly into the hole where her coffin was.

I can't write any more.

Love,
Joanna

September 14, 1974

Dear Mrs. Finney,

Congratulations on your second baby! Now you have one of each, just like Kevin and me. I bet you and your husband are really happy.

It was nice of you to write to me after Lou died. When I wrote you she was dead almost two months and I was still walking around in a fog. I think it must be easier to let somebody go if you just love them or hate them. Your letter helped a lot.

I have a steady boyfriend now. He's a really terrific guy. His name is Lewis and he's a senior, one year ahead of me. He's a whiz in science and math. I do O.K. in those but I'm best in English and languages and social studies; I've had Latin and Spanish so far, and I want to learn French, too.

I need some advice. I hope you won't mind writing again. I can't decide if I want to be a lawyer or a psychologist or a social worker. Would you tell me what the training is for social work and psychology? I imagine you know about both. My dad can tell me about law, of course. Did you have a time when you couldn't decide among different things that all looked interesting? The future looks really exciting, but scary too.

Kevin's in eighth grade now. He's really handsome and accomplished and we're all so proud of him. I forgot to tell you: a couple of years ago I finally solved the mystery of whether you still had anything to do with Kevin. It turned out that the foster care worker had been in touch with him all the time since the Simmonses, but he kept it a big secret. I guess you just dealt with adoptions, and you were cutting down your workload for some reason, so the other worker took care of it since she knew him already. Miss Daly has been writing to him, like you have to me! He needed to have that just private to himself, but when he was 12 it didn't have to be secret anymore, I guess.

I don't want there to be secrets about me. When I get married I'm going to tell my husband about my growing up. I think of it as an adventure. I hope Kev feels the same way eventually.

Sincerely,
Joanna

September 30, 1975

Dear Mrs. Finney,

Time for college applications! I'm a senior now and feel very important! Thanks for telling me about graduate school. I'm not going to decide yet. I want to go to a good liberal arts school like Antioch, or maybe one out East like Pembroke.

We're all fine here. It was good to receive your news. I feel bad about making this a short letter but Lewis is waiting for me and I have to go. We're going to dinner at his house and then to a rock concert by Crosby, Stills, and

Nash. Do you know them? I like rock as well as classical music. I guess you could call me catholic in my tastes!

Love,
Joanna

September 21, 1976

Dear Mrs. Finney,

Here I am at Antioch. What a place this is! I'm taking European literature, Spanish, French, and psychology. The kids are very varied. I feel pretty sophisticated, walking around in jeans and a sweater with these cryptic volumes under my arm.

I can't believe it's been six years since I've seen you. I don't feel I really know you now, it's been so long. But I appreciate your staying in touch on my birthday. My parents are both well. My older sister Julie is studying speech pathology at Bucknell, and Kevin has decided he wants to be a writer. He'd better learn to spell first!

Sincerely,
Joanna

December 20, 1979

Dear Mrs. Finney,

Are you still there? Can you forgive me for not answering your letter two years ago? It was horrible of me not to reply; you've been such a steady person in my life since I was less than eight years old. And you're going to think that my only reason for writing now is just because I want something.

I'm so thoughtless sometimes. I don't know whether it's

a stage everybody goes through, or whether I have some moral weakness, left over from the old days like a scar. (I should mention that I've had some therapy here at school, not a lot, but enough to know that I want to get more someday.)

I'm a senior now and graduate school applications are in. I've decided that social work is what I want to do, and I already have an acceptance at the University of Kansas City in their social work school. Lawyers have to spend too much time blowing dust from old books and trying to argue for things they don't believe in. And psychology is too intellectual for me; I'm more of a plunge-right-in person. I guess I really do want to help people, as corny as that sounds. You and Miss Briggs and the others have been more of an influence on me than I wanted to admit, and I think that's partly why I wasn't in touch. I had to make sure I really wanted to do it, that I wasn't just following your example blindly because I cared so much for you. (Whew! That was hard to say.)

Anyway, what I want to ask you is if you would put in a word for me with Miss Briggs (I hope she's still there) at the state agency. I would like to work there part time for a year as one of my clinical placements during social work school—probably during the second year. I have sentimental ties to the place. (I'm writing now because I know the slots fill quickly.) You've been in touch with me and know me as well as anyone, I think. I hope I'm not asking too much.

Love,
Joanna

So that's Joanna's story, Miss Briggs. I pass on her request to you. Unusual as it is, it seems to me well thought out; and though there is the possibility that she has some unresolved conflicts causing her to want to spend a year at the same agency which placed her, I think it more likely that this gesture is a healthy attempt to make peace with her past. Perhaps you will interview her, at any rate, and see what you make of her motivations.

I miss old K.C., especially Country Club Plaza and the Nelson Gallery. I hope you and your cats are well (how many do you have now?) and trust the agency is not suffering too badly from federal funding cuts.

With best regards,
Janet Finney

200 Alameda Boulevard
Kansas City, Missouri
January 9, 1980

Dear Janet,

I'm almost an old woman now, and I've seen many things; not much these days make me dab at my eyes with a handkerchief. But Joanna's letters did. I locked my office door and told my secretary to tell everyone I had gone for the day, and just sat for a while and meditated on the good we try to do and how sometimes we seem to succeed.

Probably she should come here for a placement. I will certainly interview her as you suggest. The fact that she is thinking about it for her second year and not her first makes me think she realizes there could be difficulties in it for her—but she may well be able to face those and master them.

I can't ride roughshod over our selection committee, but there's plenty of time, and I do think that if she's as sound as she seems to be then a word from me will help get her a place. I'm looking forward to seeing her again. She must write us a letter, and she will hear.

It is like you not to mention that you are being considered for the directorship of your own agency in Chicago—a unit much more prestigious than this one. I heard it from a mutual friend, Ruth Torrey. You must be proud; I hope you get it. With skill such as you showed with Joanna, it's easy to see why they proposed you for the job.

I'm not surprised about you, though.

Nor about Joanna.

Cordially,
Frances Briggs

COMMENTARY
WHEN PARENTS CAN'T COPE
PROTECTING CHILDREN
FOSTER HOMES
ADOPTING OLDER CHILDREN
SYMPTOMS

Being a parent is one of the hardest jobs in the world. It requires so many different qualities that it's amazing so many people manage to bring it off as well as they do. And, inevitably, some people don't manage it very well at all. Which brings us to Joanna and Kevin and their mother Lou.

We see a sad picture here: a woman who cannot care for her children properly. The full details of how Joanna and her brother were neglected are not given in the story, but Mrs. Finney gives a short description at the beginning of her letter. How can it happen that a parent, after raising a child for months or years, becomes unable to provide a good home for him or her? How does it come about that a child can be removed from the parent's home? What happens after that? And how does it work when a child past babyhood is placed in an adoptive home? These are the questions to be looked at in this commentary.

An important fact about being a good parent is that it's passed on from parents to their children. That's not to say it's hereditary, but rather that children learn as they grow up what their parents do to reassure them, to discipline them, to teach them—and if their parents' ways are successful and kind, the children will finally be in a position to use kind and successful methods when they have children of their own. Not so lucky are the children of parents who do not know how to be kind, loving, and firm; these people, grown to adulthood (like Joanna's mother), do not have good child-raising built into them. They do the best they can from what they have learned in their homes and elsewhere, but often they repeat their own parents' mistakes. You could say it is a matter of learning—a question of knowing or not knowing—but it's really more than this. Parents who were raised with reliable love have more flexibility and more strength when things are difficult, because during childhood they didn't have to worry whether to expect a kiss or a clout on the head, a smile or a sneer; their personality had the chance, without the strain of worry or fear, to grow deep and rich.

So far we haven't answered the question of how a home can become unsuitable for a child, when it was adequate before. Understanding that some parents received poor care from their own parents, you can see that in many cases it isn't a question of a sudden big change. Rather, many mothers and fathers live with a more or less constant feeling of strain and distress. When things are going right, they feel reasonably good and can be warm and loving with their husband or wife, children, and friends; but if something happens to upset the applecart, like an illness, a fight with a loved one, or some other strain, then such a mother or father feels lost and without strength to carry on. At that point such parents may have no love to give, and may be so wrapped up in their own misery that they neglect a child's needs, or even physically abuse a child who doesn't act like a loving, caring, helping person. Naturally children, having needs of their own, don't always act that way toward their parents, and that's when they tend to be treated badly by parents whose own emotional tide is at a low ebb.

In addition to parents who suffer from this kind of chronic emotional malnutrition, others have special problems. Some are alcoholic or drug-addicted. Some have severe emotional illnesses (of the kind that psychiatrists call schizophrenia and manic-depressive "affective" conditions) which cause them to have abnormal thinking, severe depressions, or periods of strange, senseless overactivity. Some have a cruel streak and behave in a depriving and physically harsh way toward one or more of their children all the time. Some misuse their religious beliefs to justify unusual or depriving behavior toward children. And some have physical illnesses which affect the way their minds function from time to time, so that their judgment and thinking are interfered with.

In any of these situations, things may be bad for a child from the start, or they may become worse, gradually or suddenly. With Joanna's mother, we get the impression that she was able to be a good mother off and on, in between periods when her children were badly fed and clothed, poorly supervised, and required to look out for their mother's health and safety. When such conditions are present in a child's home, the law in all fifty of the United States, and most of the civilized world, provides that a person observing this situation (usually a doctor, nurse, police officer, or teacher) must report it to an official organization. In the United States, that is usually the child protective service of the state department of public welfare. The department must then send someone to investigate the home; sometimes the parents can be helped by the welfare department or agencies they work with to improve the children's care, and this is always the first goal of a child protective agency: to keep children in their own homes whenever possible.

Sometimes, though, it isn't possible for the parents to make use of help, and conditions in the home remain bad, with children hungry, malnourished, cruelly treated, or not given medical attention when they are ill. In this situation the agency goes to a court and asks the judge to remove the children from the parents' home. At the hearing, usually the parents are represented by their lawyer, the child has a lawyer appointed by the judge, and the agency may also have a lawyer present. Usually the agency asks the judge to take both legal and physical custody from the parents for a certain period of time, and place it in the hands of the agency, which can then put the child into a temporary or long-term foster home or group home.

After this happens, a lot depends on the motivation and ability of the parents to change while the child is living elsewhere. Usually the parents are given the chance to make use of counseling with the hope that after six months or a year, they may then be able to do a better job. Occasionally, if extreme cruelty or neglect has occurred, the parents do not get a second chance. The laws are written nowadays with the good of the child—not the parents—considered first.

If parents show no improvement in their ability to care for a child, and a considerable time has gone by (perhaps two years or more), the question of adoption may come up. This is a big step, because it means the original parents must give up, willingly or unwillingly, their right to raise the child as their own. Foster homes are very important when a child is in an emergency situation, or when a child needs to be kept for a limited period while a family difficulty works itself out. But by their very nature they are temporary; foster parents for the most part do not wish to make the child a permanent part of their family. And often a foster child is the first to go when a foster family has a crisis of its own, so that the children's agency must sometimes look for a second, third, or fourth foster home for a child.

The foster parents' task is a difficult one, too, for many reasons. One is that many times they come to love foster children as though they were their own, yet the best place for the children may be their parents' home, or an adoptive one, and the foster parents must be emotionally ready to say goodbye and wish the children well as they leave them. It is important to mention, though, that nowadays more and more foster parents are being encouraged to adopt children who have been in their care for considerable time, when the feelings are right on all sides.

People interested in the welfare of children are coming to believe that family situations that cannot improve should be identified as early as possible to save the children from having to adjust to a series of foster homes, and so that the children can be placed in adoptive homes where they can have the chance for a family to live with permanently.

It used to be thought that only infants or very young toddlers should be adopted, because an older kid would be too set in his or her ways to adjust to what an adopting family would expect. The dangers of a child not fitting in with adoptive parents are real (and will be taken up in the commentary on the story "Something Died"). But people have begun thinking differently about the adoption of older children.

A major part of the new thinking is that many adoptive parents are willing to do without the hope that all their children will grow up to be like them in many ways, and follow a course that they set out for them. That kind of hope has been traditional for parents, and people who adopt infants often share in it. But many parents have found that it's important to let their children grow up to be what they want to be and what is natural for them. This is no less true for biological than for adoptive parents, but it's most pressingly true for parents of children whose personalities are already largely formed before they are ever adopted.

If a mother and father can be content when their son reaches close to his potential happiness, when their daughter achieves something near her native ability, without worrying too much about what line of work or what social group the child eventually moves into, that helps to make a suitable adoptive home for an older child. And if the parents are able to wait for the child to come to know and trust them, without being upset if he or she doesn't show them much love in the first year or two, that helps even more.

A final word should be said about symptoms. Joanna and Kevin had scars from their experience; she stole a great deal, and he didn't open up to his adoptive parents for a long time. These symptoms, like those of a temporary illness, faded away in time. But while they were present, they were signs that Joanna and Kevin were in a vulnerable, unstable state—that is, that things could still go badly for them if they did not receive the understanding they needed. Evidently the new parents realized that the theft was a persisting sign of past deprivation, and the lack of trust was natural, given the circumstances of the children's lives.

In former times, such symptoms might have been taken as signs of bad character, to be corrected by harsh punishment—or else as signs of inherited characteristics, uncorrectable and an indication that such a child was a poor risk. It's clear that if Joanna and her brother had been punished severely they might never have left their symptoms behind; and that if the symptoms had been taken to mean that they were poor risks and could not change, they would probably never have been adopted at all. Instead, these problems were taken along with the good parts of Joanna's and Kevin's personalities, and the prediction was made that these two kids would probably straighten out—which they certainly did.

The Assignment

Day 1: Friday

Jason McKay woke violently from restless sleep. He sat on the edge of his bed, hands clamped over his eyes to keep the images in.

"What was it? Where was I?"

A picture came back to him: a road, perfectly straight, going off into the distance. He stood looking anxiously at the faraway point where the line disappeared. Something very important was waiting at that distant place.

And that was all.

It didn't make sense. Not what he had dreamed, but that the image pulled him so. He wanted to go back. But there was only his dark bedroom with its desk, chair, and bureau, the luminous clock face that said five after two, and his barbells by the window catching the moon's light.

As he rode his bike to school the next morning Jason's

eye fell on the white line in the middle of the street. He found himself following it to see how far it went. A road, he thought. A white line. That reminds me . . .

Assignments to be handed in for Spanish, math, and biology; lunch; classwork in five subjects; and swim practice. His day's activities left little time to waste. He had lunch with Clem Rossler, Judy Gomes, and Anastasia Mavropoulos, three of his close friends. While they ate they discussed the latest project in Mr. Wall's American history course. In a unit called "The Melting Pot," everyone had to give oral reports on three ethnic groups and their contributions to American life. Then they had to learn to show family lineage, using squares for men and circles for women. In this way they had to record their own family trees going back three generations, and write as much as they could about the people named. The class had groaned when the assignment was given out.

It was due in less than a week.

The kids were shaking their heads. "Sure, families are important," Anastasia said, "but why does Wall have to make such a huge deal out of a family tree? Who needs circles and squares and lines?"

"I don't know," said Clem thoughtfully. "It could be interesting. Interviewing people and all. I wonder how far back most people can trace their families."

Anastasia smiled. "Actually it is kind of interesting. I bet I could get quite a history from my grandmother. She comes from a village in the hills in Greece, and my family says she knows about ancestors back to the sixteen hundreds. One guy had a folk song made up about him; he was a robber in the mountains, kind of a Robin Hood character. I wish my Greek was good enough to understand the whole thing when she sings it!"

That night Jason sat down to work on the project. He sat at his desk and looked up at the Ohio State pennant on the wall; his brother Bruce was a freshman, and he hoped to go there too. His mind wandered to the pleasures of college life. Then, collecting his thoughts, he tried to picture his family tree.

The first thing he thought of was a small maple tree, strangely denuded of all its leaves but one. The solitary leaf hung and blew in the breeze of his imagination for a while. He thought, There's one dead end.

Then he took a yellow legal pad and drew a series of circles and squares: his father's family on the left, his mother's on the right, with himself and Bruce hanging like square cherries on stems from the line connecting his parents.

Dissatisfied, he partly erased the stems into dotted lines. After all, it wasn't a blood relationship he and Bruce had with each other, or with their parents.

Now with a sudden irritable motion he ripped off the sheet, crumpled it, and started on a new page. He measured the sheet to find the exact center. At that point he placed a tiny square. Under it he wrote JASON in neat capitals.

The rest of the page he left blank.

Jason suddenly felt a chill. The wind that blew outside his window seemed to be coming from far away, even from the distant stars. It seemed to him his family's house was becoming very small, then with it the street, the town, the continent. Finally the world and the other planets shrank to sand grains which knew nothing of Jason or any person. He took an extra quilt to bed. As his thoughts veered toward sleep he recalled a quotation from last year's general science book. When the French philosopher Pascal learned of Galileo's discoveries about the planets and the stars and the vast distances between them, he had written: "The eternal silence of these infinite spaces fills me with dread."

Day 2: Saturday

The next evening after dinner Jason was talking with his parents about the project while they had their coffee.

"I don't know how to go about it, Dad. If I just show your side and Mom's, that's not the whole story. But if I try to show the rest of it, I'm up against a blank wall."

"Well, not entirely, Jay," his father replied. "We do have that information the agency gave us."

"But it's not enough. All there is, is "brown eyes, and likes sports," and there's hardly any information about my grandparents. He wants us to go back three generations, and that's not even two. The others'll all be writing funny stories and adventures and stuff, and if I do the adopted thing I won't have any of that. It'll make me look weird."

"Then why don't you just leave out adoption and write about Mother's family and mine? After all, it's really nobody's business that you're adopted. It isn't something you have to wave in people's faces."

"No, Dad, I don't want to make a big deal about it. I'm not ashamed of it, either. It's just a fact. But I want to do this thing right. You and Mom *are* my parents, but so were those other people, in a way." He looked at his mother for help. A comfortable-looking woman tending toward overweight, she smiled now but didn't speak. If she had something to say, she said it—otherwise you had to wait. Finally she said, "It puzzles me too, Jay. But I imagine you'll come up with something."

Day 3: Sunday

After breakfast with the Sunday paper, the McKays drifted off to separate pursuits. By early afternoon Jason had caught up with his friends in a pizza parlor where they spent an hour over sodas and pizza. When the group broke up around three o'clock and Jason headed home, he remembered the assignment.

What a bummer, he thought, as soon as I'm alone again it comes back to haunt me. It's not fair. They should let me kick a field goal instead. Or swim two hundred laps. This just isn't my assignment.

He kicked a stone and sent it flying. It landed on somebody's porch and made a racket. An old man was sitting there; he looked up and scowled, but Jason pretended not to notice.

Might as well act like a punk, he thought. Somehow this whole business makes me feel like one.

That night he had a dream.

He was walking down a road like the one he'd dreamed about before. Now there was a difference between the two sides of the road. On the left were fields, barns, signposts, houses, people; all familiar looking. They looked as though they'd been drawn by an artist for the Sunday comic section—simplified, with no shadings of color, just everything bright. But on the right side was a vast elevated stage with strange dramas being played out on it side by side. Kings and queens, a youth with a trained bear, a woman in a white Roman toga holding a baby; all speaking different languages.

Jason woke up scratching his head. The important thing about the dream seemed to be the difference between the two sides. But what was it? The left side was plain, simple, and the right side—what? Fantastic, dramatic, he guessed.

He wondered why he felt sad. Then he shrugged and got out of bed.

He began whistling a song to lift his mood, then stopped as he remembered again: that lousy assignment. What a thought to start the day with. I wish it were next week already and the stupid thing were out of the way.

Day 4: Monday

That day he performed mechanically, going to class, doing swim practice, exchanging news with friends. But he found his thoughts constantly returning to last night's dream, and to the assignment.

At lunch he sat with Anastasia. As they ate their spaghetti, Stasia looked at him. "Yond Cassius has a lean and hungry look," she quoted. "He thinks too much."

"What on earth—?"

"You look as if something's eating you, Jay. I don't want to butt in. I just thought I'd ask."

"Well, now you mention it, actually something is. You know a lot about poetry and stuff like that. Does that mean you know about dreams?"

"Well, I don't, but my grandmother does. She talks about them a lot. We hardly listen anymore, but sometimes what she says makes sense. I've even told her a few of mine."

"What does she say? When you tell her a dream, how does she make sense out of it?"

"Let's see." Anastasia ate some spaghetti as she thought for a moment. "She says a dream is a picture of a moment in your life. It could be a moment in the past, or the present, or it could be some time in the future that you're afraid of or wish for. I remember one time I dreamed about this repulsive huge toad having an argument with a beautiful pony. I thought it was ridiculous, but I told Yaya about it and she said it meant I had to make a choice. When I thought about it, it fit exactly. Stanley Parker had asked me to go out with him, and I said yes just for something to do, even though I really can't stand him. And then Jeff Elston wanted to go out with me the same night. I couldn't decide whether to break the date with Stanley. When I realized I'd turned him into a toad it seemed pretty silly to go out with him, so I told him I was sick. I always did think Jeff was cute."

Jason laughed. "That's amazing," he said, "having a real village wise woman in the house. Thanks, Stasia." And he said goodbye and went off to his next class; it was only after he'd left that Anastasia realized he had scarcely said anything about what was on his mind.

As he went to bed that night he thought he might dream again. And in fact, before long he was back on the same road. He was approaching the long stage that paralleled the right-hand side. Someone was here with him, a girl who looked vaguely like Anastasia, but like his mother too. She was urging him to do something. He called out, *Show them to me!* Nothing happened, and the girl said, *Try again, louder.* With intense longing he screamed, *Show them to me!*

The curtains on the stage began to draw apart. Suddenly he was filled with terror at what might be revealed.

Jason woke with a cry: "Mother!" He'd done that often, years before, in the days when he'd had bad dreams. He felt ashamed of waking this way at fifteen, and was glad his mother seemed not to have heard. It was barely light outside and he heard the waking calls of sparrows and robins outside his window. He couldn't get back to sleep, and lay restlessly in bed until it was time to dress.

Day 5: Tuesday

Tuesday passed with the same distracted feeling that Jason had had the day before. He worried again about the assignment. He'd become obsessed with handing it in on time, he realized. It was due tomorrow, and he hadn't written a word. Why did it matter? His record at school was at least average; one late assignment wouldn't matter. He began to see his struggle was not so much with Mr. Wall but with himself.

He looked for Anastasia in the cafeteria at lunchtime. "Stasia," he began, "could we go over that Spanish today? I can't seem to get the subjunctive."

As Jason had hoped, Stasia invited him to her house. There were always good things to nibble on there—sweet baklava, salty Greek olives, and once in a while delicious hot triangles of puffy dough with spinach inside. ("First time I ever liked spinach," he'd told Stasia's grandmother once. She had smiled at him shyly and said he should come more often so he could eat good Greek food.) He hoped the grandmother would be there today, too.

They sat in the living room and began to look at the verb forms. Then they translated a few sentences. Finally Anastasia looked at him in exasperation: "Jason, you know this stuff as well as I do. Why in the world did you say you needed help?"

Jason hesitated. He ate an olive. "Stasia," he said finally, "it's not Spanish I'm having trouble with. I didn't know how to say it. It's that dumb assignment for history class. I just can't seem to get started, and I thought you might give me some ideas. I've been having these weird dreams, too, and I think they might have something to do with it. You and your grandmother seem to be the resident wizards around here."

Stasia's eyes widened. "I love a puzzle. Let's see. Why would a guy like you have trouble with plain old history homework?"

"Well, it's not exactly plain old homework for me, Stash. Did I ever tell you I was adopted?"

Stasia looked at Jason. After a pause she mused, "Yeah, I remember. I never thought much about it though. That does pose a problem, doesn't it? How much do you know about your original parents?"

"Not much. About enough for a caption under somebody's picture in a yearbook."

"O.K. What about those dreams? Let's get Yaya in here and see what she can do with them."

Jason hesitated. "This must be a little unusual, isn't it?"

"Are you kidding? Half the Greeks in town over fifty bring her their dreams. You wouldn't be the first high school kid, either—just the first one with a name like McKay!"

Anastasia went to the kitchen and came back with her grandmother, a small stout woman wearing an apron over a cotton print dress. She smiled at the visitor; her eyes were dark and surrounded by creases. "So you have dreams," she said briskly, with a strong accent. "Eat something first. Maybe cup of coffee. I just make some good Greek coffee."

Jason smiled back, embarrassed, and accepted the offer. As he sat with the coffee and some crumbly cookies covered with powdered sugar he told his dreams: the first one, in which he had seen the road and known there was something important in the distance; the second, when he noticed the difference between the two sides; and the third, in which he kept shouting and then woke in fear.

Yaya sat listening, sipping her coffee and looking intently at the boy as he spoke. When he finished she said,

"Now I ask a question. Something happens in your life right now?"

"Well, nothing big. There's just something I can't seem to get done for school, and I'm kind of bummed out about it."

"'Bummed out' means what, Stasia?" asked the old woman.

"He means he's upset, Yaya." And then Stasia spoke in Greek to her grandmother. "I just told her what the assignment was, Jay. And I told her you were adopted, too. I hope you don't mind. It seemed important."

Yaya rose and came over to Jason. She sat down next to him on the sofa and looked at him with a grave smile. Her face got even more wrinkled about the eyes. "So. You don't know who was the woman, and who was the man. And you want to write about, anyway." She put a hand on Jason's. "You will write about, and you will write true thing about what you know, and wonderful story about what you not know. What you not know is special for you. Is hiding behind curtain on the—how you say it?—the stage. Makes you afraid, but can be whatever you want. Why not?"

But Jason had another question. "What about the two sides of the road? What do they mean?"

"Is easy to tell. One thing you know. Very simple. Bright colors. That is the parents you live with. One thing you not know. Mystery. Scares you. That is the other ones."

"What about the first dream, when there was something I really wanted, at the end of the road?"

"Is what you go to in your life. Who knows what is? Beautiful wife, children maybe. You be very smart or very rich. You get there on the road of your life, between to know and not to know. No different from anybody else!" And the old lady broke out laughing and offered Jason another cookie.

Leaving Stasia's house Jason felt like jumping out of his skin. He ran a block, then started whistling, then decided to skip. He hadn't done that since he was six.

That night he left the assignment alone. He knew it would be done before the deadline—*his* deadline. He enjoyed *Ice Station Zebra* on TV that night, and slept without dreams.

Day 6: Wednesday

Jason woke at dawn with the first light and bird-calls. After dressing quickly, he drank milk in the kitchen and left a note for his parents: "Went to do some writing before school. Jason." Standing by the table he frowned until he realized what was missing. Before his name he wrote the word *Love.* Then he gathered his papers, got on his bike, and found a place on the freshly cut grass in front of the high school. Taking a pen and a fresh pad of paper, he began to write:

"My name is Jason. I was born on November 1, 1965, and I have four parents, eight grandparents, and sixteen great-grandparents. Eight of those are still alive, and I also have sixteen living great-great-grandparents. Some of them live in monasteries in Tibet."

He chuckled as he wrote. After all, the family from the right side of the road could be anything he wanted, couldn't it?

"One of my fathers is a watchmaker, and the mother who lives with him is a registered nurse. They are great people, and taught me a lot.

"My other father has several jobs. He was once the king of Sweden, but he got bored with that and now he takes turns being a brain surgeon and a hit man for the Mafia, specializing in dockside murders. In the summers he takes time out to be a famous animal trainer with a circus, and I help him with his act.

"My other mother does several things too. In the months that have an *r* in them, she is a famous Japanese prostitute." By this time Jason's expression had broadened to a grin, and he laughed aloud. "She also works as a cleaning woman in the Empire State Building in New York, but she often likes to stay home and take care of her large family. . . ."

By now Jason's face became solemn again as he realized he hadn't once used the word *adopted*. He didn't hate the word, but to him it had an official, legal sound. He was pleased and surprised by his flight of imagination. He thought, It was as much fun as any game I've ever played. . . .

Day 7: *Thursday*

Mr. Wall had all the projects now; they were all piled on his desk by the end of class Wednesday. Jason didn't care what mark he got. But he hadn't thought about what might happen in the class discussion. Mr. Wall was a thin, rigid man with little imagination and less sense of humor, and Jason began to feel tense.

"I read your projects last night, ladies and gentlemen. I was quite impressed with most of them. But there was one that surprised me, because the young man who wrote it doesn't usually take his school responsibilities lightly. It seems to me, Jason, that apart from the fact that you didn't hand in a chart, your write-up shows such a frivolous approach that you deserve a failing grade."

He then proceeded, to Jason's extreme mortification, to

read aloud everything he had written. Jay felt the blood in his cheeks and his ears, and the muscles standing out on the back of his neck. He wanted to hit the man. With difficulty he kept quiet, saying to himself angrily over and over, He just doesn't understand.

Mr. Wall concluded his sarcastic reading of Jason's work, and asked, "Do you think that's a respectful picture of your origins, Mr. McKay? A hit man for the Mafia? A Japanese *prostitute,* for God's sake!"

Clem rolled his eyes at Judy, who sat in the next seat. They were puzzled by what Jason had written, and by the scene that was developing. He hadn't told anyone but Stasia how much trouble he was having with the assignment.

Slowly Jason rose and stood beside his seat. Everyone looked at him.

"Yes, Mr. Wall," he began in an even tone, "I think it's respectful enough in the circumstances. But respect has nothing to do with it." There was some shakiness in his voice now. "Did you ever hear of adoption, Mr. Wall? Did you ever hear of not knowing where you come from, Mr. Wall? How much fun do you think that is? I think I did pretty well with your little assignment." He sat down; his hands were trembling and his eyes were full.

There was a long silence. Mr. Wall sat down at his desk looking ashen gray. Students looked at each other uncertainly; a few tried to meet Jason's eye, but he wasn't ready. The second hand on the wall clock made a full revolution. As the tension in the classroom climbed intolerably, Mr. Wall spoke again:

"I didn't know."

This time his voice was different; no longer the schoolmaster, no longer the judge, now he sounded almost like a friend: a tired, aging friend.

"I have to ask your pardon, Jason. You should know something about me." He paused. "You should all know something about me. Now that Jason has put the matter so strongly, with such imagination, when all I've done is to avoid it."

There was another long pause, during which the teacher's thoughts seemed far away. . . .

COMMENTARY
AWKWARD SITUATIONS
RESPECT AND DISRESPECT
IS FANTASY ENOUGH?
ON NOT KNOWING WHAT TO CALL THINGS

Jason is a pretty average kid in most ways. But he becomes unusual in his classmates' eyes by refusing to take an easy way out in a situation which is awkward for him.

He didn't ask to be singled out, and he seems like a boy who would rather not stand out from the crowd. But the family tree assignment (usually given in grammar school, but occasionally later, as in this story) often has this kind of effect on adoptees: they either have to lay it all out, or else keep something a secret that isn't shameful at all. It's hard to know which way to go. (Adopted people have similar dilemmas in doctor's offices, when the doctor asks if there is any diabetes or allergy in their family background. Mostly they don't know, but hesitate to admit this because they'd have to say they were adopted, and they may not want to go into this if they barely know the doctor.)

83

Mr. Wall is an interesting case. At the end he's about to tell the class something about himself—presumably that he was adopted, too. It's ironic that he wound up teaching about family trees and origins, and putting so much emphasis on respect for one's ancestors. Ironic, but perhaps not altogether strange, because that was *his* way of dealing with the problem of origins. We might even guess he would have agreed with Jason's father, who suggested that Jason forget about presenting the biological side of his background. Wall might even have understood Chris Miller's parents and their frightened attitude in the first story. They all lean toward what David Kirk calls "denial of difference"—that is, the attitude that being adopted, or being an adopter, is no different from being "home-made" or being a biological parent living with home-made kids. Jason knows better. Even though he doesn't feel sorry for himself for being adopted, he knows there are differences involved.

About the word *respect* that Mr. Wall seizes on: has he picked up, correctly, on an undertone of anger in Jason's fantasy? There's a certain power in being able to turn your original parents into anything you want, including various kinds of low-life individuals, as Jason did, and maybe part of this is a revenge motive for their having abandoned him. Probably the teacher and Jason are both right. There really is disrespect here, in a narrow sense. But as Jason says, "Respect has nothing to do with it." Maybe he means he shouldn't be required to feel respect toward parents who didn't keep him, whatever their reason; maybe he means that to picture them as a pile of different possibilities is as far as he can go for them, and also the best way he can get things together for himself.

Will this fantasy be enough for Jason in later years? Or will he try to forget the whole thing, or else become a searcher like Chris? We don't know. It used to be thought that the less satisfactory an adopted kid's home life was, the more likely he or she was to seek additional information or make an actual search. More recently, students of adoption are finding that although this pattern may be accurate to some extent, there are many exceptions to it. Many people who are quite close to the families they grew up in still feel a need to learn more about their birth parents, or to seek them out.

But no one would have a right to criticize Jason if he continued to leave things right where they are at the end of the story—keeping his adoptive parents as the known, and keeping the other side unknown, mysterious, threatening, but full of promise.

As Yaya says in the story, "What you not know is special for you." All of us, adopted or not, have private dreams and hopes and fears. These secret forces—if we use them judiciously, and don't let them take us over—can be terribly important and useful for us in the way we conduct our lives.

Jason's difficulty with the assignment is part of a set of problems faced by many adoptees at various times in their lives. These all relate to the general question, "How do I present my adoption to people outside the family, and what do I call my adoptive parents and my birth parents when I talk about them with my friends?" This question makes us look at the way people use language, and how language is connected with changes in social customs. We might call this part of the discussion, "On Not Knowing What to Call Things."

The language people use is sometimes very precise and clear (as in a scientific paper), and sometimes deliberately vague and suggestive (as in certain poetry and novels).

Language can also be clear in an ordinary way (as when someone says, "Please shut the door!"), or confusing because the speaker has not chosen his words carefully enough. ("Mary, what happened to my thing for the whatchamacallit?")

One kind of confusion in speech comes about not because of any fault in the speaker, but because the language we use reflects social customs and habits, and when social change and confusion occur (as they are occurring in large measure in this second half of the twentieth century), the words for certain things can't be any clearer than the customs they describe.

Take for example the way social change has affected the way people refer to blacks, women, and homosexuals. Thirty years ago in ordinary polite speech people used to refer to a black person as a Negro, and to a woman as a lady; a homosexual was called a homosexual, if referred to at all. In those days, to call a Negro *black,* you pretty much had to be black yourself; to call a lady a *woman,* you had to be careful you weren't insulting her by implying she wasn't ladylike; and the general topic of homosexuality was banned from polite conversation and for the most part was whispered rather than spoken about.

Now all that has changed, and the rights of all these people have been aggressively defended, with the result that the way they are spoken about is different too. *Woman* and *black* are the most common terms now, and many people use the term *gay* for a homosexual, following the preference of some members of that group. People who use the old terms may find themselves quickly corrected. Even someone who tries to write an article, or a book like this one, has to be careful not to give offense by writing in a male-oriented way, as almost all writers were accustomed to do when writing for a general readership. If I wrote only *he* and never *she* when talking about some unspecified person, I am sure some readers would think I was unfair leaving out the girls and women. (I would write *he or she* more often than I do, if I didn't think it made sentences unnecessarily long and awkward.)

What has all this to do with adoption?

There are a number of problems about the words that are available to talk about adoption. For example, what does an adoptee mean by the word *parents*? There is sometimes the question of which parents are being referred to. And what tense of the verb does the adoptee use when talking about parents the adoptee has never seen, and has only bits of information about from some years in the past? Does an adopted girl say "I know my father [here meaning birth father] was six feet tall," or "is six feet tall"? If she says "was," does it mean she thinks he's dead, or just that she can't picture him being six feet tall *now* because she has no recent knowledge of him? The small packet of information sometimes available to an adopted child too often comes to resemble a snapshot, taken at a moment in the lives of the birth parents; since the information is rarely brought up-to-date, the young adopted person has trouble picturing the birth parents developing and growing into maturity, but may imagine them as perpetually young adults without a clear direction in life.

Another semantic problem (that is, a problem related to what words mean or don't mean) is what adoptees call themselves after they're no longer children. "I'm an adopted child" is accurate as long as the speaker is a child, but might sound odd coming from a fifty-year-old company president. Many adoptees continue to be referred to as adopted children or to use that phrase of themselves well into their adult life, simply because *adopted person* does not come easily to their tongues, and *adoptee* sounds too clinical or legal (perhaps too much like *amputee*!) to be used comfortably. And change is needed in this usage of words, because referring to people who are not children as children is regressive and demeaning. Where is the basic difference between this situation and the habit, many years ago, of thinking of black people as overgrown children and calling them *boy* or *girl*?

It should be remembered that many tribes that are referred to as primitive have extremely complex vocabularies to describe different kinds of family relationships—vocabularies that would put ours to shame. It's not that adoptive situations are too confusing to have clear names; if African Bushmen and people in other preliterate societies can be clear about their relationships in speech, then surely we can learn to be clearer about ours. The only reason adopted people still suffer from the lack of clear ways of talking about themselves and their relationships is that social custom has not kept up with their needs. And just as other groups have managed to bring about changes by making lots of noise, so can adoptees and their friends.

Some of these language problems could be helped if people carefully thought out the issues involved and promoted the use of certain words and expressions that accurately express the situation. Other problems (like the *is* or *was* dilemma) can't be solved easily, and may never be solved, at least not as long as our social structure keeps birth parents and adoptive families separate.

Hormones
Have No Color

When Larry Silver was seven years old he went with his family to Nassau during Christmas week. The trip was especially memorable to him for the exotic flowering poinsettias and other plants, the many odd tropical fruits, and the strange colorful birds with names like *bananaquit* and *ani*.

He also remembered it because of something that happened on the beach one day. He and his parents and his sister Jessica had been walking across the hot sand toward their beach chairs when they saw an old white-haired man looking at them. Larry had seen him in their hotel.

The man smiled at them as they passed in front of him. He looked at Larry, then at his parents. Then he said, "Is he your adopted son?"

Larry's father, used to such questions from strangers, smiled neutrally and nodded: "Yes indeed."

Suddenly the man pinched Larry's earlobe and smiled at him in a frightening way, then, turning, said loudly to his parents: "A little black boy! You people must be crazy." Then he wandered off over the beach.

Larry looked at his mother's face, then his father's, for guidance or instruction. His mother looked blank, as though stunned; on his father's face he saw rage appear like the sudden clouding of a summer sky. His father clasped him tight and said in a shaking voice, "That was a sick man, Larry. Sick and bad, too." Jessica, two years older, had been the least upset of all. She said in her matter-of-fact way, "Well, Daddy, you're a doctor. You should know about sick people. It's just too bad he brought his germs to *this* beach!" And they had burst out laughing, and the clouds had gone away, and they all went swimming and then had a bicycle ride before lunch.

After that, within the family, the old man became a symbol for a kind of reaction that some people had to Larry. When the four of them were on the street or in a store or moviehouse, it often happened that someone would look at Larry's dark skin and curly hair, compare him with the rest of the family, and look surprised. Usually the person would then pass on with no other reaction, or else would smile at them; but sometimes a mean look came over the person's face, and more than once they heard muttered words of hate. When that happened one or another of them would say, "There goes the old man from Nassau!"

By the time Larry was fourteen he was finishing his freshman year in high school in Lexington, an old New England town near Boston. He was an average student, but he shone in sports and had a hobby that took up much of his spare time. He had a ham radio operator's license and his bedroom was cluttered with electronic equipment: diodes, capacitors, wire cutters, transistors, and special postcards called QSL's from all over the world with the call numbers of people Larry had spoken to. Like most ham operators, Larry treasured these personal tokens of long-distance conversations. There were cards from twenty-five of the fifty states, as well as from England, France, Finland, Saudi Arabia, Liberia, Venezuela, and Barbados. They were ranged around the mirror above Larry's bureau, stuck on carefully with Scotch tape; this arrangement, in fact, was the only perceptible order in the room. He had his own QSL card too, printed in bold type:

LARRY SILVER
122 RANDOLPH ROAD
LEXINGTON, MASSACHUSETTS 02173
U.S.A.
w12zk3

Dr. and Mrs. Silver had lived in the same house since Larry was a baby. The doctor was a quiet, studious man who disliked arguments. His wife was lively and liked parties and fancy dinners. They made an odd pair, perhaps, but their marriage was a good one. They and Larry and Jessica were part of the neighborhood, and no one paid particular notice to the fact that Larry was black. Perhaps the only person to think deeply about it was the rabbi of their temple. At thirteen Larry became the first black youth ever to read in Hebrew from the Scroll of the Law in the ceremony called bar mitzvah. It moved the rabbi to give a brief talk about friendships between different races in ancient times, and about human brotherhood.

During spring vacation this year Larry was spending his time shooting baskets with some neighborhood friends and talking on the radio. One day he was listening at random on the amateur band and heard a young man's voice:

"CQ, CQ, I'm talking from Roxbury, A13FT9, anyone listening? A13FT9 monitoring. Go."

Roxbury is the part of Boston where most of the city's black people live.

Larry, who had talked to people ten thousand miles distant on his radio, felt an odd sense of remoteness as he heard this voice, as though he had suddenly tuned in on a distant mysterious land. With some excitement he responded to this voice only fifteen miles away:

"Roger, A13FT9, this is W12ZK3 in Lexington. I read you. Over."

"Loud and clear, W12ZK3. That Massachusetts or Kentucky? Over."

"Massachusetts."

"Shucks, you're just in my backyard, over."

"A13FT9, what's going on in Roxbury? Over."

"Kids playin' basketball, people walkin' down the street. What's your name, man?"

"Larry Silver, funny man. What's yours?"

"Othello Stanton. Like the Shakespeare play. You in school? Over."

"Freshman, Lexington High School. How about you?"

"I'm a senior at Jeremiah Clarke High School, play sax in the band. Why don't you call me tomorrow? I'm usually on the air between three and four, over."

"You got it, Othello A13FT9. Nice to contact you. Talk to you again. Clear!"

Larry turned off his receiver-transmitter. He felt eager for tomorrow to arrive so he could talk to this black youth in Roxbury again, whose voice bore the cadences of black people's speech as Larry's did not. How could he have learned to speak like that, he reflected, with two Jewish parents? True, Mother and Dad had several black and intermarried couples as friends, and some of these people took an interest in the boy. But they were doctors, lawyers, and writers who lived mostly in a white world. Often Larry had thought something was missing from his experience. Could he find it in Roxbury? His father occasionally drove him through the area on the way to the hospital where he worked. On those rides he looked out at the kids playing on the street and enjoyed a sense of secret kinship with them.

The next day he called Othello on the radio, and was elated to find him on the air. They talked almost every day for a week. Then one day Larry announced at dinner, "I'm going to Roxbury next Saturday."

Mrs. Silver was serving peas. She looked surprised. Her voice was tight as she asked, "Is it a school trip, Larry? You didn't tell us about it."

"No, Mother, it's just something I want to do. There's this high school senior I've been rapping with on the radio. We have some interests in common, so we thought it would be fun to get together. He invited me to have lunch with his family and look at his radio setup, and maybe play some ball with him and his friends."

Larry's father looked serious. "You going in on the train?"

"Thought I would, yeah, then get the subway to Dudley Station. And then a bus. He told me how to come."

"You better let me drive you, Larry. It's not always so safe there."

Larry knew how busy his father usually was on Saturday, and suddenly he began to feel as though he were struggling for breath. The air in the room had become heavy. He sensed, in his mother's controlled silence and his father's protective offer to drive him, some violation of his own rights. He tried to identify what he felt, to put it into words.

"Hey, I should be able to go into Roxbury, shouldn't I? I mean, I'm black, aren't I?" His voice was loud, his heart was beating rapidly, and he felt a flush enter his cheeks. Everyone was silent for a moment. Larry had spoken with more anger than he realized until he heard his own voice resounding in the room; now he was hot with embarrassment.

Quietly Dr. Silver said, "Lawrence, go to your room."

Larry knew injustice was being done. "Sure, I'll go to my room. And stay there, too!" He walked off heavily, breathing hard, and the three people left at the table could hear his door close firmly and the bolt slide in the lock. The three white Silvers sat looking at their tuna salad and peas. Then Mrs. Silver looked at her husband, but he did not meet her glance. Finally Jessica spoke:

"Daddy."

"What, Jessie?"

"I think maybe Larry has a point."

Taken aback, Dr. Silver looked at his sixteen-year-old daughter. "What do you mean?" he asked, trying to maintain control.

"Well, Larry *is* black, you know, Daddy. And he wants to go to the black part of town. Is that so strange? Then you tell him that the black part isn't safe. How do you think that makes him feel? He takes it personally."

"I don't know, Jess. I have a headache. Help your mother clean up." Without speaking to his wife or looking in her direction, the doctor stood up, wondering what had happened in the space of three minutes to make his head spin so badly.

"Can I finish eating first? At least *I* still have my appetite."

"Mel," his wife said, "maybe we overreacted. Sit down, dear, and finish your dinner." But he left without a word.

Mrs. Silver sat there uneasily while Jessica cleaned her plate and had a wedge of apple pie from the bakery.

Larry took the train to Roxbury that weekend and was tingling with excitement. The unpleasant episode with his father was momentarily forgotten. He had traveled half a dozen times or more into Boston, alone or with friends, but never to his present destination. He got off the train at South Station and took the MBTA subway to Dudley; from there he took the Blue Hill Avenue bus to Quincy Street. The trip took an hour and a half in all.

As he walked along he noticed a curious thing. He was aware that the farther he got into Roxbury, the more something that he usually carried with him fell away— something like caution, or being on guard. It was like not noticing the sound of the refrigerator motor until it suddenly stops. People smiled and nodded at him as he passed. And he quickly realized that, because almost everyone was black, he was not doing something that he habitually did every day of his life: he was not keeping a watchful eye open for the old man of Nassau. The feeling was exhilarating.

When he found 286 Quincy Street he noticed a girl of about his own age scrubbing the stone steps of the three-decker house. She smiled at him when she saw him hesitate: "You must be Larry. Come on in. I'm Othello's sister, Ruth. He's up in his room." But there was something in her glance, cordial as it was, that Larry couldn't figure out; she looked surprised, he thought, and puzzled.

"Othello, come on down. Your friend's here!" called Ruth. And down the stairs, two at a time, ran a tall, athletic youth with medium brown skin and an Afro. When he saw Larry he stopped in his tracks, his mouth open, and suddenly he burst into laughter. Extending his right hand to Larry, he clapped him on the shoulder with his left. "Larry Silver! You didn't say you was a *brother*! And with a name like Silver I told everybody I was gettin' a visit from a Jew!"

Larry looked cautiously at Othello, a twinkle in his eye. "You are," he said quietly. The three of them were silent for a moment. Then Othello quipped, "Anything can happen in a place like Lexington, Massachusetts." He started laughing all over again; then all three burst into laughter.

Mrs. Stanton emerged from the kitchen. She was a tall woman, dressed in skirt and blouse, with a pleasant, businesslike manner. "You must be Othello's friend from Lexington. It's nice to have you here. My husband is at work, but if you're around later on you'll meet him." She told Othello and Ruth where she had left the food for lunch, and excused herself to go to her job.

The afternoon was one long amusement park ride for Larry. He felt as though he were in another country altogether, and did not, at first, let his new friends know that he had never before been in a working-class Afro-American home. He was attracted by Othello's quick wit, his relaxed manner, his knowledge of radio, and most of all by his ready acceptance of Larry as a younger colleague and friend. Ruth impressed him, too. She was quieter, with lighter skin than her brother, but she shared his good humor and her eyes were large and warm.

Larry had to leave to get home in time for the family dinner hour; guests were coming. Just as he was leaving Larry met Mr. Stanton, a tall, serious-looking man with a moustache who worked for the telephone company. He arrived home in work clothes. He put an arm around Othello and gave him a squeeze, then did the same with Ruth. Then he shook Larry's hand firmly and invited him to return soon.

Larry's third visit to the Stantons, in June, was to be a sleep-over. There were plans for a block party with music, dancing, and food; Othello had a steady girlfriend, and Ruth, to Larry's surprise and delight, had asked him if he would be her escort.

That evening Jessica was out on a date, too. Dr. Silver and his wife were sitting in the comfortable living room of their restored two-hundred-year-old house. He was reading the *New England Journal of Medicine,* and she was looking over a French novel; she worked as a translator for publishers of modern fiction.

Dr. Silver looked up from his journal. "Beth, I think we're losing him."

She glanced up and returned to her book. "Casey the gardener? No, dear. I told you he's in Ireland visiting his parents. He'll be back in July." They had been discussing the garden shortly before.

"Not Casey, Beth. I mean Larry. Our son, the one who lives upstairs."

"Melvin, what in the world do you mean?" She put her book down with a resigned sigh, certain that whatever was about to begin would mean at least half an hour of work lost.

"I don't like Larry going into Roxbury. I'm sure those people are nice, but when he comes home I notice a difference in his speech. He sounds almost uneducated. I don't like how easily he lets himself be influenced."

"Mel, we don't *own* Larry. And when we said we'd raise him to have some knowledge of being black, surely that didn't mean only letting him meet the black people that *we* knew, did it?"

"Well, of course not. But he's in there now and he's on a date, at fourteen. Who knows what he'll get into? Drugs, drinking, sex—"

Beth Silver rose from her chair and went over to the

couch where her husband sat. "Hormones have no color, Mel. You've talked to him about sex, and we've both talked to him about love and marriage. He could get involved with a girl just as easily in the suburbs as anywhere else, and make the same mistakes as he could anywhere else. As far as drugs and drinking are concerned, I have a lot of confidence in his judgment."

"I'm not convinced. I just feel he's slipping away."

"Just what you said when Jessie was fourteen, if I remember right. Please lay off the boy, Mel." She put her hand on his head and ran it through his graying hair.

Her husband was silent. After a moment she seated herself again. The breeze blew the odor of honeysuckle from the garden into the room, and Dr. Silver picked up his magazine and proceeded to read the article he had begun.

It was about hormones.

Late in the summer Othello and Ruth were invited to dinner in Lexington. First there was swimming at the pool-and-tennis club, then drinks at home. (Ruth and Larry got ginger ale, and Dr. Silver, after some hesitation, offered Othello a beer, which he declined.) Mrs. Silver had prepared a cold supper of sliced turkey, roast beef, and raw vegetables with home-made garlic mayonnaise, to be eaten with French bread. This was one of her favorite warm-weather meals. Her famous cheesecake and coffee followed. The conversation was lively, and Jessica, who had not met the Stantons before, pronounced herself charmed by them. When Othello and Ruth had been driven home, the family went into the living room and Dr. Silver sighed in satisfaction as he sank into the sofa. He did not notice the alert look on Larry's face as he waited for his father to pronounce some sort of judgment, as he invariably did on meeting someone for the first time. Nor was he aware that Larry was mentally reviewing the doctor's reactions to his trips to Roxbury over the preceding months.

"Nice kids, Larry. I admire your taste."

Larry waited.

"They both seemed quite bright, I thought. It's a little hard to tell, though, because they're not trained to express themselves verbally in exactly the same way we are."

Oh, shut up, Daddy, Jessica thought. She prayed that her father would suddenly be seized by a fit of coughing so prolonged that he would forget the topic. But it was too late. Larry was on his feet.

"I've had enough of your condescending attitude," he shouted at his father, his eyes moist and his voice unsteady. "You always have to say something to put them down. You don't *want* me in Roxbury, and you don't want Roxbury here!"

Dr. Silver stood up, looking grim. "Listen, young man. Your mother just entertained those two kids with a feast, and we took them swimming before dinner and just drove them all the way home. They're your friends, not ours. Is this the kind of thanks we get?"

Larry took up the challenge. Stepping close to his father, he suddenly noticed for the first time that he had grown taller than Dad. He was big for his age, and Dr. Silver was a bit under average height. The suggestion of a physical advantage added fuel to the fire. He saw his father as an enemy, a patronizer of blacks, a user of Larry.

"You're damn right. You know what I think? I think"—and now Larry held back a sob, pausing a moment—"I think you don't *like* us very much. I think you're prejudiced, like the old man in Nassau!"

The physician looked at his wife and daughter sitting there, silent appeals to him on both their faces. It had always been hard for him not to take things personally. This, he knew, was a moment when it could be disastrous if he took offense at his son's outburst. He sat down.

"Larry."

Larry remained standing, his arms at his sides, his fists clenched as though ready to take a swing, his breathing rapid. He didn't answer.

"Larry, please sit."

Between guilt and anger now, Larry sat down. Having mastered himself, his father went over to him and cautiously placed his hands on Larry's head, then gently pulled it so that his abdomen was a pillow for Larry's tears. His son did not resist.

"I don't think it's really about race, Lar. I've been pretty pompous about Roxbury since you met Othello, I guess. But I think it's really something else. Jessie, do you remember when you went out on your first date?"

"Do I ever remember you that night," said Jessica. "I thought we should cart you off to Westborough State Hospital. You really had a lot of trouble with it, Daddy."

Mrs. Silver was smiling. Somehow, Mel had managed to come through. Larry stood up, his eyes shining.

"You just don't want me to grow up, is that it, Pop?"

"I think that's it, Larry. But I really don't think I can stop the process."

"Thanks, Pop."

Mel and Beth Silver looked at each other and grinned. They climbed the stairs to the second floor, leaving Larry and Jessica in charge of downstairs. These two soon settled down to a game of Monopoly, helped along by a large plate of leftovers from the last supper of Larry's childhood.

COMMENTARY
ADOLESCENCE
TRANS-RACIAL ADOPTIONS
IDENTITY
STIGMA

Larry's story introduces two themes: one is the growth and the struggle for independence that are typical of the teenage years; the other is the idea of identity, including the special situation of children who don't belong to the same racial group as the parents who raise them. Toward the end of the story, there's a question as to which of these themes is more important. Larry and his father are both finally relieved to realize that what looked like race prejudice cropping up in the doctor was really the reaction of a man to his son's growing up and moving gradually beyond his control.

Not all adoptive parents think very much, when they take an infant or young child into their homes, about the time when that lovable bundle will become an awkward, self-contradicting, rebellious, and perhaps pimpled person a dozen or so years later. For that matter, when any parents dream about having a baby, the adolescent period of the child's life is rarely what comes to their minds first. What needs to be said about adolescence in adopted kids is that whatever storms and agonies nonadopted teenagers go through with their families, the adopted ones go through the same—only more so. (There's some evidence that certain adolescent adoptees may be more passive and compliant than the average, but this isn't the general rule; these kids may in fact be more troubled than most, and may be showing it by being afraid to live active lives.) Adolescence is a time of great testing. Kids worry whether they are strong or smart enough, whether they're lovable, whether anyone really cares—and they often manage to provoke people in a dramatic way. What they're really doing is trying to make sure that no matter how obnoxious they act, their parents still love them; no matter how unattractive they make themselves, their parents still find them attractive.

Imagine, then, an adopted person of this age, who may always have carried around a little invisible banner that says "Prove that you love me! My first parents didn't keep me and I'm not 100 percent sure you will either." Add to that the confusions of the teenage years, and sometimes what you get amounts to an explosive mixture.

Teenagers are often troublesome to their parents—but from their side, they often feel their parents misunderstand them. Sometimes a kid makes parents feel very proud, and at other times provokes them to the point of anger. What many teenagers find most valuable in a parent is a kind of constancy or reliability. A parent with this quality will not try too hard to be a pal, and will remember that the parent and the son or daughter belong to different generations—but will be friendly most of the time, and will not lose control very often even though angry. These characteristics add up to the kind of *maturity* which is supposed to go with being older, and which kids have a right to expect from parents.

What about trans-racial adoptions?
They have been talked about a great deal by child welfare experts and by the general public. The questions people ask about them usually have to do with something called *identity*. "How could a black child growing up in a white family have a healthy sense of identity?" some people ask—and with some reason on their side. What is this mysterious *identity*?

It's something important enough for us to consider, important for everyone, whether white or black, child or adult.

Webster's International Dictionary defines identity as "the condition or fact of being a specific person or thing; individuality." The dictionary goes on to define "identity crisis," a concept which is also of interest: "the condition of being uncertain of one's feelings about oneself, especially with regard to character, goals, and origins, occurring especially in adolescence as a result of growing up under disruptive, fast-changing conditions."

What identity means, for our purposes, is the group of feelings, thoughts, and beliefs that a person builds up gradually about himself or herself. These come as a result of what the person learns about his or her personal history and background from parents and other sources, and from what he or she discovers about his or her own individual personal qualities from the reactions of family, friends, and others. A child finds out that he or she is short or tall, stocky or slender, dark-skinned or light, robust or prone to illness. A child learns what ancestors did, where they came from, and whether any of them was well known and respected for good deeds, or imprisoned for crimes. And a child discovers that others see in him or her a person who is lovable and interesting, or dull and deserving of neglect. All these facts and ideas go into a child's personal sense of identity.

If the picture of self that the child builds up out of all these different brush strokes turns out to be a pleasing one, he or she is well equipped to take the ordinary risks of living without feeling like a permanent failure or reject if a piece of bad luck arises. But if the picture is flawed, if the person it shows is not satisfying to the child's own eyes, if there seems to be no harmony between the human figure and its painted background, then the child may be in for confusion, depression, or other trouble.

Identity can be national (Irish, Italian, Swedish) and religious (Catholic, Protestant, Jewish); these are forms of identity handed down within families. Then there is the identity one feels as an American, let's say, when watching Fourth of July fireworks, or singing the Star-Spangled Banner at a baseball game, or when traveling abroad. There is the identity you get from your family: most teenagers feel connected to what their parents do for a living, what kind of house they live in, what the family does for fun, and where they go for vacations. All these are forms of identity that we did nothing to earn; we came with them already attached, so to speak. (Or I should say most of us did, for when a person is adopted it's a bit different—but I'm getting ahead of my story.) Then there is the identity one earns, usually from a combination of native ability and hard work—for example, being an expert tennis player, a mathematics whiz, or an Eagle Scout. And there is negative identity: the girl who does poorly in school, the boy who never learned to catch and throw a ball well, the dwarf, the stutterer, the child born with a missing hand or a deformed leg.

Another word for negative identity is *stigma,* and there are various kinds of social stigma, too. Society often looks down on people who are in prison, and sometimes their children are regarded as different from others. In another context, members of certain minority groups are denied the right to buy houses in certain neighborhoods or are not hired to work for certain employers.

You might ask at this point whether being adopted, in itself, might carry a kind of stigma with it. Or, for that matter, if being an adoptive parent carries a stigma. Judging from the amount of energy adopted people *and* adoptive parents sometimes use up in *denying* that there's anything different or disadvantageous about adopting or being adopted, I would have to say that the answer is yes, adoption *can* carry negative meanings, at least within some people's minds, or else they wouldn't be spending so much time denying it! And some adopted kids have the strong feeling that their friends and associates see them as different, or as unfortunate souls, or something of the kind—even though the friends might not have actually said anything.

So how can being adopted get in the way of forming a comfortable identity, a relaxed and confident sense of who you are? Let's look at this more specifically before turning to trans-racial adoptions.

The simplest way to put it is that it makes a big difference to a kid growing up how his or her mother and father feel about being adoptive parents. If they weren't able to have their "own" child, this was probably a loss for them, and they need to get over the loss and move on—otherwise they may remain a bit uncomfortable about adoption, like Chris's parents in the first story.

Whatever their reasons for adopting, they have to learn that an adoptive family (even one that has "home-made" kids in it) is just a bit different from other families, mainly because adoptive families are still a small minority, and many people feel a tiny bit of surprise or even confusion when they learn that a friend or acquaintance is an adoptee or an adoptive parent. Coping with these little moments of surprise in other people is one of the main things that makes an adopted person, or an adoptive parent, feel slightly out of the mainstream.

If parents never become fully comfortable with the idea of adoption, their kids may grow up with the idea that they're not fully comfortable with *them.* They may feel rejected, and may in turn reject their parents and their parents' way of living. But some of this is normal for all teenagers, and adopted teenagers often reject their parents' values even more than other kids—perhaps because they're not sure these values are really *theirs,* and they wonder from time to time what values and lessons they would have learned if they had grown up with their birth parents.

In this discussion, we've dealt with several of the things that affect the way a boy like Larry grows up in his family. One thing has not been mentioned so far, however, and it is perhaps the most important. That is the fact that the child's birth group—in Larry's case, black people—have a society and a culture of their own, to which the child may one day want to belong. People like Larry's parents, if they adopt a black child (or a mixed-race child, whom people in the United States will probably regard as black), should prepare the child to live as a black person if he or she chooses to, even though the adoptive parents are white. This is not an easy task, and some people believe it is an impossible one.

Several years ago an organization of black social workers published a statement that opposed trans-racial adoptions. They reasoned that such adoptions are unnecessary, since many or most black infants born out of wedlock are raised by relatives, and said that these adoptions reflect unfavorably on black people, making it appear that they cannot take care of their own children in need. The social workers also raised the question I have referred to above: how can a white family give a black child black identity? There is no clear, common agreement among adoption workers on this score, but many adoption agencies and families have taken matters into their own hands, believing strongly that trans-racial adoptions can work. They say that what is most important is for the parents to try to provide the child with substantial links to the black community, and then leave the child room to forge his or her own identity upon the anvil of experience.

THE GHOSTS IN THE BOX

Van pulled and tugged at the old trunk and finally got it to the middle of the attic floor. His father had given him an ultimatum: "Clean up your corner up there or we'll throw everything out." He had gone on to say that now Van was twenty-one and engaged to Debbie, it was high time he got rid of his old Boy Scout uniforms, bug jars, comic books, and so forth. "Mother wants to use it as a studio, and she can't until you reduce that mess drastically."

So there Van was, up in the cold attic after dinner, while the snow fell. He wasn't too keen on the task; he would rather have been waxing his skis in preparation for tomorrow's trip to Mount Killington with Debbie. He was on his last Christmas vacation from Amherst College, where he majored in Asian studies. He planned eventually to go into the U.S. foreign service.

The trunk bore a large mailing sticker:

> VAN DINH MURRAY
> CAMP PASSUMPSIC
> BARNET, VERMONT

It was not locked. Van opened the latches with growing interest; he'd half-forgotten what lay inside. The layer of dust on the lid testified to the years gone by since the trunk had last been disturbed.

Within, on the top, lay old high school notebooks: biology, trigonometry, American history, carefully labeled in block lettering. Shouldn't throw these out, he thought, leafing through them with only partial memories of the contents. Then a shirtbox containing his high school projects: the genetics of fruit flies, a senior paper on "Colonialism and Its Effects on the American Character." He noted his opening sentence:

> I find it odd that the available textbooks go into great detail about American interests in Panama, Cuba, Puerto Rico, and the Lesser Antilles, but make little mention of the widespread condescension of the American people towards China and the rest of the Orient, expressed in the phrase "white man's burden."

Van smiled. How angry he had been then! The years between, he thought, had been spent in learning to marshal and direct that anger.

He was content to explore the trunk at leisure. Downstairs his parents were watching television; "Masterpiece Theatre" was doing a Shakespeare series. His younger brothers were both occupied. Gene, a freshman at Colby College in Maine and also home on vacation, was out with his long-time girlfriend, and Doug, the baby, had just gone down to lift weights in the basement, where he would be good for at least an hour.

Next out of the coffer came photographs. There were pictures of the wrestling team, snapshots of friends, and one of Van and his date at the Junior Prom. He was beginning to get bored when he saw an eight-by-twelve spiral notebook with SECRET written on the cover in thick red letters; he felt his heart beat strongly. Half-remembered lines of poetry flashed through his mind. Leaving the other articles on the floor, he carried the notebook down the attic stairs to the kitchen, where he fixed himself a large glass of iced tea with lemon, and, thus equipped, he went back to the second floor. He sat down in an overstuffed chair in the room he shared with Gene, switched on the lamp, and began to read:

> My name is Van Dinh Truong. I am twelve years old. They call me Van Murray but that is just my American name. I have been in this country for two years. Before that I lived in Vietnam. I have learned good English.
> Tôi tên là Tru'ong Dinh Văn. Tôi muoi hai túôi. Má tôi mât rôi. Ba tôi mat roi.

As he read of his parents' death in the old language, he felt his eyes fill up. How brave I was, he thought. And for the thousandth time he practiced remembering the last time he had seen his parents.

Van had developed memory into an art form. It began when he moved with his family from the village of Rach Bap, in Binh Duong Province, to Saigon, just after his sixth birthday; he earnestly wanted to keep in his mind the picture of thatched houses in neat rows, Buddhist roadside shrines, rice plants in the wind, farmers with conical hats carrying panniers on their shoulders. The city was different. He could not roam freely because of the dangerous traffic, and his father, having risen from the post of village schoolmaster to that of a minor government official, could not spend as much time with him as formerly. "*Má tôi,*" he would say, "my mother, help me remember." And she would sit with him and paint word pictures of their old life; she, too, missed it, though she enjoyed the shops and boulevards of Saigon.

One day his parents left him in the care of his grandmother, who had come to the city with them and shared their apartment. They told him at breakfast that there was a big American drive to conquer the National Liberation Front in Ben Suc and Rach Bap, and that the Americans and the ARVN troops were destroying property in an attempt to root out Vietcong. They were worried about their house, which they had left partly furnished, and about the safety of cousins whom they had left living in it. "We are going only for the day," they told him. "We'll get a car, drive up and get our relatives and whatever we can take with us from the house. It may be a bit crowded here for a while when we get back. You need not fear, the roads are safe, and the people in control of the area are our friends."

Van had cried when they kissed him goodbye; he did not like this journey. To ease his mind, as the day wore into late afternoon, his grandmother recited many verses of the old narrative poem *Kim Van Kieu,* from which he himself could already quote at least thirty lines. Soon she reached these, usually among his favorites:

> When I leave for the Kingdom of the Nine Springs
> You will never again see my face nor hear my voice . . .

Van looked up at his grandmother's face and begged her to stop reciting. The lines reminded him of his parents' departure. They sat in silence through their supper, and did not sleep until late. It was three days later that they learned Van's parents had been gunned down by soldiers in a helicopter. They had been having a picnic lunch near the road; it seemed the soldiers had mistaken them for Vietcong.

His grandmother tried to keep things going. She moved them to a one-room apartment and sold most of the furnishings of the larger one, even some of her son's books and treasured old manuscripts and pictures. The two of them began a grieving, threadbare existence in a neighborhood full of bars and cheap hotels. Van often used to gaze at the few of his father's hanging scrolls his grandmother had found room for on the walls of their room. It was as though they held some clue to his parents' sudden disappearance from his life. He imagined that if he could somehow read the strange characters displayed on them, it would serve as a magic spell to bring his parents back.

Six months later his grandmother was stricken with paralysis; she was unable to rise from the bed one day, and when she tried to speak it came out as an alarming gabble that he could barely understand. Van ran in panic to the traffic policeman stationed at the corner, a block from their apartment. He arranged for an ambulance. Van saw his grandmother placed on a stretcher and lifted onto the vehicle. He jumped in, over the attendants' protests, and persisted in staying with her as she was taken to the hospital ward.

When after four hours Van still would not leave the ward, the nurses called the doctor in charge. He was a young man with a moustache, who looked a bit like pictures of the national leader, Colonel Nguyen Cao Ky, that Van had seen in the newspaper. He spoke kindly to the boy: "Your grandmother has had a stroke. The flow of blood to a part of her brain was cut off during the night, and it has left her unable to move or speak normally. It happens to old people often. She will be sick in bed for a long time—weeks, perhaps months. She is worried about you, and asked that I arrange for you to be cared for. You will have to go to a children's shelter." Van went to kiss his grandmother, who responded with a weak, sad smile; then numbly he allowed himself to be led by a nurse to her automobile, and driven to a large house on the outskirts of Saigon. Above the door was a large sign in Vietnamese and English: CHILDREN'S HOME OF THE VIETNAMESE RED CROSS SOCIETY. He was taken to see his grandmother in the hospital once a week. She gradually recovered her clear speech and most of her power of movement, but remained weak on one side.

After two months his grandmother was discharged from the hospital, but she did not return to their small apartment. She was still too weak, the doctors told Van, and needed to rest further in a home for elderly people who were recovering from such illnesses as she had. "Will she ever come home?" asked Van, but he received no answer. When he visited her in the nursing home and saw her walking he was shocked at how badly she still limped and how thin she had gradually become; somehow while she was still in the hospital he had not noticed. She told Van, "I am too old and sad to make a home." So he stayed in the children's shelter and she stayed in the nursing home, and they took turns visiting each other.

More than two years passed. Van was treated decently in the home, and because of his intelligence and enthusiasm he became a leader of the children and a favorite of the adults who ran the place, the administrators and teachers. He was now nine and a half; he could read and write well, play the guitar, and speak some English and French. One Sunday his grandmother took him on an outing to the center of Saigon; they traveled on the streetcar, and got out at a public park, where Van played while his grandmother sat. Then she took him to a small restaurant where, over bowls of rice with *nu'ớc mắm*—a spicy fish sauce—and cups of tea, she told him her plan:

"You know how sick I am these days. Twice this winter I have had pneumonia, and I never got back the full use of my right arm and leg. It is all I can do to go out on the streetcar as we did today; when I return I will be very tired. How can I bring you up as your parents would have wanted? I cannot make a home for you. I cannot pay for you to be educated. And all the relatives who might have helped are either dead or wounded, or living behind enemy lines—not only on your father's side, but on your mother's, too."

Van did not know what was coming next; he fingered his teacup nervously.

"I am afraid of what will happen in this country, Van. If the Front wins the war, things will be very different here."

"What are you thinking, Grandmother?"

"Van, many Americans are inviting children from Vietnam into their homes to become their sons and daughters. Your parents liked the Americans; your father often told me he would like to visit the United States. Perhaps you can go instead, and one day return here if it is still possible."

And so Van first learned that he might go to live on the other side of the world. He was angry, sad, excited, amazed. Confused by the whirlwind of his feelings, he refused to be sent out of the country while his grandmother still lived. But they agreed between them that she might begin to make inquiries about a home for him overseas.

Within the year she had passed away; a third, more severe chest infection proved too much for her weakened body to withstand. One day, shortly after her funeral, Van found himself in the office of the director of the children's home. There was a family in America interested in adopting him.

Van stood in the middle of the worn carpet in the director's office, aware that he was expected to be pleased with this news. He closed his eyes briefly and recited to himself silently the first five lines of *Kim Van Kieu*. It was a trick he had taught himself, to keep his mind balanced when events were moving too fast, and he was feeling threatened. Then he asked, "Please explain to me 'adopting.'"

The director told him that a married couple in the state of New Hampshire, far away on the Atlantic coast of America, wished to have him as part of their family. They already had two sons, younger than Van; he would be the oldest. The man would become his father, and the woman his mother.

"But that is impossible. I had a father and a mother; I remember them every day. How could these people love me when I am already a big boy? How could I love them and obey them when I have never seen them?"

"They can educate you, Van, better than you are likely to be educated here; they have money to pay for it, and they say they have much love in their home for another child, even one your age."

"But I am Oriental, and they must be big-nosed white people! How could I be part of their family?"

"In America such things are done, Van. I am told that it often works out well."

Van stood his ground. In the children's shelter he knew and was known by everyone. He had a place, and was respected. He had long since stopped expecting love; instead he gave and received friendship and loyalty. Love, he thought, could wait until he was grown and would have a wife and children of his own.

Every day for a week the director called Van into his office. Each time Van stood on the rug, gazing at the floor in front of his feet, and said nothing. The director did not know what to do with him. Finally he had an inspiration.

"Van," he asked the boy, "you are from a Buddhist family, aren't you?"

"Yes, sir."

"So am I, although I have some Confucian relatives and a Christian wife. Do you know the legend of the Four Signs?"

"Everyone knows that, sir."

"Could you tell it to me? Come, sit in this chair."

Van so loved the old stories that he forgot for the moment why he was in the director's office. He began, proud of his knowledge:

"The Lord Gotama lived in the house of his father the Raja Shuddhodana in Kapilavastu, surrounded by luxury. His father wanted to protect him from the knowledge of pain and evil, so he would not be tempted to give up the throne when it came his time to rule. So he gave him everything he wanted, hoping to keep him inside the park that surrounded the house.

"But Lord Gotama became bored. One day he asked his charioteer to harness the horses and drive him to the edge of the park. There they saw a wrinkled, weak man who walked with a stick. 'What is the matter with that man?' asked Gotama, and the charioteer replied, 'He is old, my lord.' 'And will I too grow old?' 'Yes, my lord, no one has yet found a way to escape it.'"

The director was filled with pleasure at Van's expertness in telling the tale, but was careful not to let it show too much. "Good, Van. Go on."

"So Lord Gotama asked to be driven back to the house to think awhile. And his father asked the charioteer what had happened, and he told him, and the Raja said, 'We should give him more nice things, and more young men to be his friends and pretty young women to be his companions, so he'll stay close to home.'

"But one day he wanted to go out again, and this time he saw a sick man who had fallen on the ground and could not hold his urine. And the charioteer explained sickness to him, and he went back and thought some more.

"And another time they went out and saw a funeral procession and Gotama saw death, and learned that it too touches everyone. And he thought a third time. And finally they took another ride in the chariot and saw a man in a yellow robe with a shaved head. Gotama asked the man who he was, and he answered: 'I am one who has gone forth.' And Gotama didn't know what this meant, so he asked him. And the man said, 'I have gone forth to seek for the truth, and to harm no living being, and to discover help for those who suffer.' And Lord Gotama said, 'Truly you have gone forth. I, too, will go to have my head shaved, and will wear the yellow robe and go forth as you have to seek help for those who suffer.'

"So the Raja's plan didn't work, and Lord Gotama left home and sought wisdom for six years. Finally after many trials and failures he determined to find quickly what he was looking for. He sat under the Bo Tree near the river Nairanjuna for forty-nine days and forty-nine nights. He sat with fierce intensity, tormented by the Evil One, but at the end of that time he had discovered the Four Noble Truths and the Eightfold Path."

The director smiled gently at Van. "That was told beautifully. Can you guess why I asked you to tell it?"

Van was silent. An idea was forming in his mind. The director waited, and at length Van said, with a grave excitement, "The Buddha had to go forth from the place where he was living, to gain wisdom. You think I have to do the same thing."

"I do, Van. You love Vietnam as I do. But I have had my education, and it is hard for me to see how you can get yours here, with things as unpredictable as they are. You are very bright, you know; with you I speak as I do to boys three years older. To waste that would be a pity. I don't think the Americans are any wiser than we are. But they have peace in their country, and they have much to offer: schools, universities, and professional training."

"The Americans killed my parents, sir."

"They may have done so, Van. We don't know whether an American or an ARVN soldier was manning the gun in that helicopter. One thing you will learn is that there are stupid people in all countries, and cruel and bloodthirsty ones as well. You will learn too that many things happen in war that make no sense at all. No one can ever make up to you the murder of your parents; but perhaps the American family named Murray can give you the training you need to do good in the world."

Later that day Van was introduced to the representative of an international agency which would be responsible for him during the first year of his placement with the Murrays, and he was reassured that if things did not go well, the agency could protect him, and even change the arrangements if it were necessary.

Finally Van gave his consent to the journey and the adoption. His tenth birthday came a few days before he was scheduled to leave on the plane. There was a celebration in the orphanage; the director had arranged for a traditional Vietnamese puppet show, and there was sherbet, and a cake with eleven candles—one for good luck. The party was loud and boisterous, with much singing. But after the happy songs, the teacher who sat at the old upright piano began playing "Auld Lang Syne." Some songs are international, and this traditional Scottish farewell was known to the children, who sang it to Vietnamese words. Van was so well liked that many cried as they sang, teachers as well as children. And of them all, the director had the wettest cheeks. In front of all the others, he put his hand on Van's head. "Never forget your family and your life here. Let memory be your sword; sharpen it every day. Keep your mind prepared. You must never lose what you have seen and what you know."

Van had one large suitcase to hold his clothes and the few books and toys there was room for. He had a separate case for the old manuscripts and pictures that had been his father's. These, plus a few photographs, were all that was left to Van of his parents, and he treasured them more than any of his other possessions. The writing on them was in the old style, in Chinese characters, unlike the modern way of writing Vietnamese in Western letters. Van hoped one day to be able to read them and learn what secrets they might contain. And the small guitar with which he had entertained the orphanage children had to come, too. When the time came to leave, Mr. O'Neill, the social worker from the International Red Cross, insisted on carrying Van's suitcase for him, and reassured him in other ways.

Mr. O'Neill was the first red-haired person Van could remember seeing. When he first caught sight of this huge, broad-shouldered man he was struck by the sight; Van thought he was wearing a flamboyant wig. He had a gentle smile that said, *I know you're sad and scared, but there's a lot to look forward to.*

He was driving an old black Citroen. In the front passenger seat Van saw a frightened-looking little girl holding a teddy bear. She said her name was Cuc; she was six years old, and she was going to new parents in New York. She didn't know any English, so Van amused them both by teaching her to say "good morning," "thank you," and "please give me some Coca-Cola."

The plane ride was long and tiring. There were changes in Honolulu and San Francisco, and crowded air terminals to walk through. Van felt important; since Mr. O'Neill spoke scarcely any Vietnamese, Van could be the one to interpret what was going on to little Cuc.

At last they arrived in LaGuardia Airport in New York, where they were met by Cuc's new parents. Now it was time for the last part of Van's trip—to Hanover, New Hampshire. Van had studied the map and knew they would be flying north, almost to the Canadian border. For a moment, he was afraid Mr. O'Neill would leave him to make the rest of the trip by himself. But the big flame-haired man took him for a hamburger and promised that he'd travel with Van until they met the Murrays in Hanover.

"But you have family. You have children. They probably mad you away so much time."

"They know what I'm doing is important, Van." Just then the hamburgers arrived. It was a new experience for the boy. He bit into his, looked thoughtful for a minute, and said, "Taste good. But not taste like pig!"

Mr. O'Neill broke out laughing: "It isn't pig, buddy. It's cow."

Van looked at him in surprise. "Cow work in field. Have so many cow here you eat them, too?"

O'Neill laughed again. "You bet your life we do. Americans wouldn't know what to do without beef—that's what we call cow meat. But don't worry, there's plenty of pig meat here, too!"

They took the shuttle plane to Boston, and connected

there with a flight for Hanover. On the way, Mr. O'Neill explained that Mr. Murray taught Oriental languages at Dartmouth College, and his wife was an artist who made weavings and beautiful clay pots.

"You see them? You see their house?"

"No, but another social worker who lives in New Hampshire met them and wrote to my office with lots of information about them. And they have two children."

"I know about children. Two boys more small than me." Van was wondering how the two boys would take to the idea of having an older brother suddenly imposed on them. He thought he might have to choose whether to be meek and quiet, and have them think he could be pushed around, or else come on strong, and risk making a fool of himself. On the flight to Hanover he thought about it some more and decided the most sensible approach would be to act friendly but reserved, and keep his guard up.

The Hanover airport was small. Only a handful of people waited for arriving passengers in the late afternoon sun. Summer was ending and the chill of fall was in the air. Many of the people on the plane were young men, who Mr. O'Neill explained were probably students at the college where Mr. Murray taught. Van saw an athletically built man with glasses and a moustache, and a slim, pretty woman in a blue dress; with them were two small boys wearing T-shirts and red caps with the letter *B* on the visor.

Peter and Stella Murray were introduced to Van. He shook their hands seriously. They introduced Van to Gene and Doug. Then there was an uncomfortable silence, as though everyone were wondering, *What do I do next?*

Mr. O'Neill had been present at such scenes before. He took charge and began talking enthusiastically about the trip he and Van had made. He explained to Van that the

B on the boys' caps stood for a baseball team in Boston. He gave some papers to Mrs. Murray, and explained that these were Van's health records. Mr. Murray stood and listened, puffed on his pipe, and smiled. Gene and Doug came over to Van, and after a moment of shyness Gene took over: "I'm Gene, and I'm seven, and this is Doug. He's five, and he doesn't know a lot."

"I do too know a lot, you nerd!" Doug looked upset. "I know about dinosaurs, and all you know is baseball!"

Van felt at home immediately. A lot of his time at the orphanage had been taken up with mediating quarrels between the younger children. "Hey, Doug, maybe you find dinosaur, then Gene teach it play baseball!" The three of them burst out laughing.

And that was the beginning of Van's life in New Hampshire.

He entered the fifth grade, and found there were two other Oriental students in his class, a boy and a girl. Both were Chinese; one was the son of an engineering instructor at the college, and the other was the daughter of a family who owned a restaurant. But Van felt lonely when he learned that there were no other Vietnamese in Hanover. One day, after he'd been there two weeks, Mr. Murray made an agreement with him.

"Listen, Van, I have a problem, and maybe you can help. You know I teach languages at the college: Chinese and Japanese. But I want to learn Vietnamese, too, and there's no one here to learn it from. Do you think you might have some time to help me out?"

Wow, thought Van. I was afraid I'd forget how to speak it. "I think we make deal, Dad. I help you Vietnamese, you help me English, maybe kids in school not make fun when I talk."

It took him a while to get used to American food, and

sometimes he longed for the pungent taste of *nu'ớc mắm* and the sweet flavor of lotus fruit. But he enjoyed watching his new mother preparing the food, and working at her weaving and pottery. It reminded him of his own mother whom he hadn't seen for so long. He could still remember her working in their kitchen in the village. And she, too, had liked to create beauty: she did watercolors of flowers, birds, trees, and fields of rice.

School wasn't easy at first. In the orphanage Van had been special because of his talents and his personality. Here, his sense of humor and skills in sports and schoolwork were not what many students and teachers first noticed about him. These people, instead, seemed to make him special because he was Vietnamese and an orphan, or because he'd been adopted into a family that looked so different from him. Van resented it. He knew his English would improve with time and there was nothing he could do about his Oriental appearance or his family situation. These were not the important things about *him*, he thought.

Van's loneliness, those first years in Hanover, had many sides. There was the small, ignorant band of bullies who seemed to assume he was related to the Chinese restaurant owner, and kept threatening to beat him up if he didn't get them free egg rolls after school.

There was the student teacher who asked Van to talk about his "war experiences" one day when the class was doing social studies. He felt self-conscious and embarrassed; he resented being put on the spot in front of his new friends, and didn't want to talk about his private griefs and adventures before the whole class. He stood there, shifting from one foot to the other until the regular classroom teacher took him off the hook. She announced that, unfortunately it was time to begin the day's math work, and if Van felt someday like telling the class about Vietnam, everyone would be glad to hear what he had to say.

Then there was the gap between himself and the Murrays. With Doug and Gene there was no problem. But the man and woman were hard for Van to get used to. They gave him clothes and a new ten-speed bike; they seemed to like him. But Van couldn't escape the feeling that they wanted something from him, and he didn't know what it was.

So he did twice the number of chores they assigned to him, but that only made things worse: his new mom asked why he was working so hard. "Do you think you need to do extra work because you're living here in our home?" He didn't know what to say. Eventually he set up a wall between himself and them to keep the tough questions out, and he spoke to them only when they spoke first.

He would go to bed night after night with an aching, sad feeling that he didn't understand. Finally one evening, as he was trying to sleep, he overheard a conversation between Mr. and Mrs. Murray. They were coming upstairs, speaking softly, but his door was partly open.

"Van seems mad at us all the time," he heard Mrs. Murray say.

"You know, I don't think it's us exactly," Mr. Murray's deep voice replied. "I think he's mad that we're not *them*— the parents he lost. We can't expect him to love us right away. He lived so long as a survivor, taking care of himself, and now here he is in a family again, after seeing all that death and destruction. I think we must remind him of his own mother and father, and he doesn't quite know what to do with us."

As Van lay there he felt tears come to his eyes. It relieved him to know that these people understood something about what he was feeling, and he drifted off to sleep.

He was so far from his own people. As beautiful as New Hampshire was, it had no rice paddies, no water buffalo, no farmers with cone-shaped hats; and sometimes Van felt furious at the fate that had brought him to a place where he never heard his native language spoken. (Mr. Murray was giving it a good try, but he pronounced things in such a funny way that it didn't really count.)

Among Van's earliest recollections were his memories of the holidays during his first year at the Murrays'. He had been there less than three months when he began hearing about turkeys and Pilgrims. There was an awkward scene when Van turned away from the dinner table, heavily laden with holiday foods, and stalked to the room he and Gene shared. No one knew what to do until Gene went after him:

"Van, come on! My father's going to say grace and carve the turkey!"

"Leave me alone!"

"Hey, Van, what's the matter? Mom tried to make everything extra nice for your first Thanksgiving!"

"This American holiday, Gene. Not for Vietnamese boy." And Van had stubbornly refused the meal; he stayed in the room all evening, and they had to eat without him.

Christmas wasn't so bad. Van had learned about it when he was small, and in the orphanage they had celebrated it, so he let himself enjoy the gifts he got, and gave some in return. He missed the celebration of Tet; no one even knew what it was, and he had to tell them about the most important holiday of his country.

But the fireworks really came on the Fourth of July. The Murrays had been to a cookout at the house of some friends, and after dinner the older boys began lighting bottle rockets and Roman candles. In the midst of the fun Van demanded to be taken home.

"But why, Van?" Mrs. Murray asked. "Don't you feel well?"

Van's English was better by now. "This is holiday for Americans who went to Vietnam and killed people, my parents, too. I don't want to be here while people celebrate." There were tears in his eyes. Mr. Murray took him home and returned to the party, but when the family came home later that night Van was gone.

No one slept that night, and by four A.M. the police were notified. The family was sick with worry. Peter Murray said to his wife, "I shouldn't have gone back to the party with him in that state. I should have stayed home with him."

Early in the morning Doug and Gene searched in all the hiding places they knew, without success.

Life went on like that three more days and two more nights. Peter and Stella got little work done and the boys couldn't concentrate on anything. Finally, at seven-thirty on the morning of July 7, the Murrays were sitting around the breakfast table when they heard a faint knock on the back door. Stella went to open it.

There was Van: filthy, with torn clothes, covered with scratches and mosquito bites. He held himself stiffly erect, like a soldier, but his eyes were dull and he seemed exhausted. No one said anything for a minute. Then Van said faintly, looking at the floor, "If you want me to stay here I stay. But you not expect me to be happy with you about American flag. Some of me still over on other side of the ocean."

Doug didn't understand any of this except that Van looked awful and he was immensely relieved to see him. "Van," he said, "here, take my chocolate milk."

Van was so hungry he took it without a word, turning away as he drank to hide his face. Then he went upstairs to bed and slept until the following night. Stella bathed him while he slept. No one ever asked where he had been.

By the time he'd been at the Murrays' for two years he'd come to accept that he was living as an American, and he might as well enjoy it, at least a little. It was around this time, when he was twelve, that he began keeping a diary in the spiral notebook with SECRET on the cover. He wrote sometimes in English and sometimes in Vietnamese. After all, he was a Vietnamese living in America, and an American boy who had come from Vietnam.

Van didn't really know he'd been accepted by the other kids until an incident late in the spring of his eighth grade year. The class had organized a hayride to celebrate their graduation from junior high school. A boy named Frank, who had never been a friend of his, came up to Van after the straw-filled wagon had come to a stop at a pizza joint and all the boys and girls had jumped out.

"Hey, chink!"

Van looked at the boy with distaste. "What's the matter, big-nose?"

Frank's face flushed. "I saw you in the wagon with Stephanie. Keep your hands off. She's a white girl, and she likes me."

"If she likes you so much how come she wasn't sitting next to you?"

Frank had trouble containing himself. "Listen, chink. Who asked you to come over here in the first place? You're not welcome here. Just keep away from Stephanie or you'll see what happens."

By now, everyone in the class had gathered around. Van said, "Who's going to show me?"

Frank punched Van square in the face. Van's cheek smarted from the blow, and his nose ached. He fell back, but quickly got up and came at Frank, feinting with his right and landing a swift blow to the midsection with his left. Frank doubled up and fell.

The hush that had fallen over the group lifted, and kids began yelling:

"Get him, Van!"

"Punch the creep, Van!"

"He's got it coming!"

The girl Stephanie stood with her mouth open, alarmed. She had long blond hair and wore dungarees and a red sweater. She had been lounging next to Van all the way to the pizza joint; he'd put his arm around her shoulder, to which she'd made no objection. She seemed to have no special investment in Frank, judging from her amused expression when Van delivered another punch, this time to the jaw.

Frank sat on the ground and held his face tenderly. He looked up at Van and muttered, "I'll get you, chink."

Van replied, "Come get me, wise guy. Here I am!" And he held his arms away from his trunk, opening himself up tauntingly for a punch.

But Frank still sat, still spent from Van's blow to his abdomen, and the others laughed at him. Van and Stephanie and the others went into the restaurant and ate, and Frank stayed outside. When the time came for the ride back to town, nobody could find him.

One day in the spring of his sophomore year in high school Van was rummaging quickly through his closet, searching for a missing tennis racket. He noticed a large, flat black case leaning against the left-hand wall. It had been almost covered by hanging clothes that were seldom used. He remembered his father's scrolls, books, and pictures, and he stood in the bedroom, torn: his friends were waiting for him outside, but the black case called to him. Finally he spied the racket in another corner of the room; he went to join the boys, but first put the case on his bed where he would be sure to see it when he came back.

He had not once opened it since his arrival in the Murrays' home. At first it was because, when he first came to America, he couldn't bear to look inside the box. He had magical thoughts about it. When he looked at it in his closet, he would have a strange, wild thought: *If I open it, my parents will be in there.* The hope and terror of that fantasy paralyzed his will. But he thought about it less and less, and by the time he was twelve or thirteen he had almost forgotten the case was there.

Now, at fifteen, Van remembered the ghosts again, but he asked his father that night after dinner:

"Dad, there's something I want to look at. But I want you to be there. Do you have a few minutes?"

Mr. Murray was protection against the ghosts.

"You mean that box of yours, don't you?"

Van looked at him, amazed.

"Well, I knew you had it when you came, and you never talked about it all these years. It's been in the back of my mind."

"It's been in the back of my closet!" They both laughed.

So Van got the box and put it on the dining room table. Together they undid the ivory hooks that secured it. Mom and Doug and Gene stood by as Van opened the flaps and exposed the contents.

On top were manila envelopes that Van knew contained photographs. "I want to look at these alone first, O.K.? Let's go on." And underneath was exposed the first of a half-dozen paintings on ricepaper, mounted on simple mats. Van remembered them vaguely as his mother's which used to hang in their house. Beneath these was a long, flat wooden case. Van slowly removed the lid of this inner container, conscious of four pairs of curious eyes. Inside were hanging scrolls, a dozen of them, each rolled tightly around a bamboo cylinder.

Peter Murray took a scroll at random unrolled it, and stared at the characters a long time. He hung it from a hook on the wall.

"That's some of the finest calligraphy I've ever seen!" he exclaimed. Van couldn't stand it any longer. "What in the world is it, Dad?"

"It's a poem by Tu Fu, Van. Eighth century. Probably the greatest Chinese poet of all time." He spoke slowly and quietly, almost as though he were in church. "It could almost be a commentary about your life." Mr. Murray sat down in one of the dining room chairs, facing the room. Stella, Doug, and Gene stood to one side, uncertain how far they could intrude on what was happening between Peter, Van, and the scroll on the wall.

"I'll try to translate it for you:

"Every day on the way home from my office
I pawn another of my Spring clothes.
Every day I come home from the river bank drunk.
Everywhere I go, I owe money for wine.
History records few men who lived to be seventy.
I watch the yellow butterflies
Drink deep of the flowers,
And the dragonflies
Dipping the surface of the water
Again and again.
I cry out to the Spring wind,
And the light and the passing hours.
We enjoy life such a little while,
Why should men cross each other?"

Van listened to the last lines and his thoughts wandered to the absurdity of war and killing.

"You know," he said, "the old guy was right." He started out talking to his father in a reflective tone, but as he went on he looked at his mother and his brothers, and spoke to them too. "It's really important to enjoy life as much as we can. But sometimes that's hard to do. Things get in the way."

"You mean like wars and stuff," said Gene.

Van said nothing.

They all stood there for a minute. Then Doug said, "Seems to me you've done pretty well at not letting it get in the way. You've come a long way from that ten-year-old gook. Nobody could tell you from Sylvester Stallone now!"

The word *gook* was always a signal for a wrestling match. It never really bothered Van, coming from Doug; he knew where he stood with him, just as he felt secure about his place with all the Murrays. Van looked up at his brother with a half-smile. Doug was five years younger but two inches taller, muscular, and roughly the same weight. Van went for him and took him down, then got him in a half-Nelson near the dining room table while Mrs. Murray watched fearfully. Doug reversed their positions and got Van in a chicken-wing. Van yelled for mercy, more for the furniture than for himself.

Peter Murray looked at the other scroll. He told Van that the writing was in Chinese, the language cultivated in the Vietnamese court at Hue for many centuries.

It was then that Van first conceived the idea of becoming an Oriental scholar himself. Whatever he used it for, he knew he wanted the knowledge Mr. Murray had, to be able to read these mysterious characters, to breathe the air of ancient poets who wrote of friendship, love, and loss.

At college in Amherst he met Debbie, who went to

school at Smith in Northampton, not far away. They met at a dance. Debbie was majoring in politics. She had brown hair and blue eyes, and read constantly when she wasn't bicycling. She had strong ideas about the United States and how the country should behave in the world. Van fell in love at once. By the fall of his senior year Van knew he wanted her to be his wife, but he didn't know what her parents would think of her marrying an Oriental, a war orphan, a person with no roots.

Fearful of rejection, one day Van hinted at marriage to Debbie. She looked at him quickly, planted her hands on her hips (they were walking on a beach at the time) and said, "Are you proposing a corporate merger, Mr. Murray?"

She was taking several business courses that term. Van picked up her terminology. "Well, kind of—but the outcome might not resemble either of the parent corporations."

"I think it's worth the risk. I've always believed in international cooperation. And I've always thought it could lead to beautiful results."

And so did her parents, when they went to talk to them the following week.

Van did not finish reading the notebook that night. He had been remembering his parents, his grandmother, the *Kim Van Kieu,* the director, the legend of the Four Signs, and his first years in Hanover; his head was too full.

Putting the book on his table with care, he thought with a wry smile that he hadn't even begun his clean-up job. Then he went downstairs to join his family. He had a feeling the skiing that vacation would be superb.

Commentary
ROOTS
SPECIAL WORRIES
GETTING ESTABLISHED
NAMES

Van's story could stand for the stories of a lot of adopted children. His has a real war in it, with bombs dropping and peopled killed. But many other boys and girls who join new families have other kinds of war stories. There are tales of oppression and poverty in Central or South America. There are the wars of a child's spirit to stay alive and hopeful through years in group homes in this country and abroad. There are the terrible battles within families that some kids have to live through until they find relief outside. But most of all Van's story is meant to show how a young person can leave one place, go to another place far away, and still remain undefeated and strong.

In the stories so far we've had a look at how some adopted kids struggle with the feeling of belonging in families they were not born to. We paid special attention to the idea of people knowing *who* they are (what their "identity" is) and how that can feel a bit different if they are adopted. The part of *you* that comes from being your parents' son or daughter is mainly the part that's different, because if you're adopted you know that somewhere else there were (or there are) two other people who actually gave you life. So it may be hard to feel altogether like your parents' child. You may be keeping a part of yourself in reserve for those others. If we want to be mysterious we can call them the unknowns. And if they're unknown, that might mean part of yourself is unknown too—perhaps unknown and exciting, perhaps unknown and frightening, maybe some of both.

For children who come from a group within our country that's different from the society the adoptive parents live in, the job of finding their place can be harder. We saw that in Larry's story. And for someone who comes from far away, like Van, fitting in is harder still. Let's make a list of some of the problems:

1. The person probably looks different from the adoptive family, and people may make remarks about it.
2. He or she may arrive speaking another language and have to go through the difficult process of becoming fluent in the language of the adoptive country. The new language may never feel quite right.
3. He or she may know nothing at all about the original parents and their relatives, and what kind of people they were.
4. The adopted child may have very little knowledge about the country of birth, the food they eat there, and the music, history, and customs that his or her birth parents knew. Besides that, the child may be mixed up about whether he or she *wants* to know any of these things. It may seem simpler to just say, "I'm an American."

5. If the person ever wanted to look for the birth parents, it might be very hard or even impossible, if records are not kept carefully in the country of origin or if there has been social upheaval or war there. Besides, it would be expensive because of the travel involved.

It might help a little to realize that feeling rootless is something that afflicts a great many people these days, particularly in countries to which there has been much immigration, such as the United States. In fact, it is unusual for an American to be able to trace ancestry back more than a few generations, or know more than one or two facts about great-grandparents. (In contrast to this are certain areas of Europe, Asia, Africa, and the Pacific, where certain communities have remained more or less undisturbed for centuries; in such places it is quite common for a person to know a great deal about ancestors going back six or seven generations.)

So you might say that most of us in America are cultural orphans to some extent—though some much more than others. (The popularity of Alex Haley's book *Roots* several years ago, and the TV show based on it, demonstrates the enthusiasm American blacks felt when they saw it might be possible to reconstruct a black family history.) But adoptees, and especially those who come from other countries, are the most dramatic cultural orphans we have.

How important is it to know your origins? And what can an adopted person do about it?

There are some things that parents are advised to do which are probably a good idea—like exposing kids to whatever they can of the country's history and culture. As children are growing up they may seek out books for them to read, or introduce them to people who grew up in their country of origin. If an adopted girl was born in India, they may take her to an Indian restaurant from time to time. But there's no magic in this. She may find she doesn't like Indian food. And when she hears the waiters conversing in Hindi and she can't understand a word, she may feel really strange: she realizes they're as foreign to her as though they were Albanians or Ethiopians. Her waiter might even make a fuss over her if he finds out she's from India. But he's not her real father, and he can't take her home.

Some cultures, such as Spanish-speaking ones, are more accessible to Americans, since many people here learn Spanish, and Chicanos and Puerto Ricans have had an influence on American life. But exposure to Hispanic culture, while important, may still not go too far toward helping a kid's dislocated feelings if he was brought from Colombia at age six and had to learn English in a hurry. He may have forgotten all his Spanish, in his anxiety about fitting into a new environment, even though people might have tried to keep it alive!

It is important to do these things together—if only because it demonstrates that parents respect a child's country of origin, and that they respect him or her as a person whose origin is in that country. They are particularly important if the child was old enough to know and remember the country's customs and language when he or she came to this country, like Van.

But sometimes these links with the culture are not enough. A boy or girl may have other worries, other thoughts: How can I get the other kids at school to treat me like one of them? How are my original family doing back in Cambodia? What happened to my baby sister, and where is she living now? These are tough problems. Some of them, like getting accepted by classmates, can be worked out pretty well over time. Others may remain as nagging worries, and there may be no way to get the information the young person is longing for.

The most important thing this kind of adoptive family can do is to say to itself, "We are a family, even though some people might not think we look like one. We have our own idea of what a family is." In a good family like this, the parents and other family members realize that life is more complicated in some ways for the adopted child than it is for other children. They have to listen to the child, and take his or her worries and griefs seriously.

After all, if a boy has a baby sister and has no idea where she is, no one could expect him to forget about her! The best he can do is to hope she's being cared for well, and to pray that one day they will meet again. He may find that he worries less about her as he gets caught up in his new family life. And then he may catch himself up, feel guilty, and say, "Wait a minute! I can't feel comfortable here! These people aren't my real family! My real family is scattered and miserable, and I have to be loyal to *them*!" One problem is that he himself probably can't do much for them now. Maybe his adoptive family can find out where his sister or other family members are. But if he wants to stay loyal to his original family, probably the best thing he can do is to get himself educated and grow up as a person with interests and skills. Then, when he gets to his early twenties, he will be in a position to go out and look for family members or to fight social injustice wherever he may see it.

This is the course Van takes. After an initial struggle with accepting the Murrays, he settles in, but he keeps a part of himself—the Vietnamese part—in reserve. For a long time while he's growing up, he doesn't know what he's going to do with that part. But he writes angrily about American foreign policy when he's in high school. Then when he goes to college he forms the idea of entering the foreign service. And the part that belongs specifically to the Orient eventually clicks in when he understands the compelling beauty and importance of the poetry of Tu Fu—even though it's in Chinese. (Perhaps one day he'll revive his Vietnamese too. Whether or not he does depends only on whether it's important to *him*.)

A final word about identity: in the story, the Murrays don't try to change Van's name to George or Alex. They let him go on being Van. Now Van is a perfectly good Vietnamese name, but it sounds sort of American (two movie actors are named Van Heflin and Van Johnson). What if his name had been Nhung or Hiep? Should they have stepped in and given him an American name that everybody in school could pronounce easily?

Boys and girls coming from other countries have to change a lot about themselves. They have to wear new clothes and learn a new language. They have to get medical examinations and sometimes get treated for infections that are common in their countries. It seems only fair that they should be able to hold on to the name they've always had, no matter how hard it is to say. After all, the name stands for the individual. If a kid *wants* a name change after six months or a year, it should probably be allowed. But if parents want the name changed to an American one as soon as the kid arrives, it might be a sign that this family can't accept the boy or girl as someone who has lived an important part of his or her life in another country. It's sad for parents not to have been in on a kid's first years—but they can't erase those years by pretending they never existed. And they must remember that those years are important to their son or daughter, and will perhaps seem even more important in later life than they do now, when the kid is trying his or her best to fit in.

SOMETHING DIED

Philip Whelan, journal entry

December 20, 1974

I'm going to write about Jacqueline as honestly as I can. Maybe if I try to remember the whole chain of events, I won't feel so much like crying, or breaking something—or driving like hell to that foster home and grabbing her in my arms so she can share Christmas with us once again. I could do that, but it would just confuse us both. And it wouldn't change a thing.

Obviously, Jackie is no longer with us. I hope she's happier where she is now. Putting it that way makes it sound as though she's dead, which she certainly isn't, thank God. But it sure felt like something died the day we finally decided, Sally and I, that Jackie couldn't continue to live in our house; *her* house too—the one she had lived in for fourteen years, since she was six months old.

I know the feel of death from my tour of duty in Korea. I remember Heartbreak Hill. This is different, but somehow it's the same—the heartbreak part, anyway.

I've put some other things into this record, too: letters from Sally and her mother and Jackie, and pages from Jackie's diary that she left behind. I sent the diary on to where she is, but I read it first, though I don't like to admit it. I know why I did: I was looking for some way to understand. I copied some of it on the Xerox machine at the office. I think it was partly a way to hold on to her, too. (I've gotten to be kind of a nut about assembling written records, actually. I got Sally to ask her mother for the old letters she'd sent her, and she gave me those, and her mother's letters to her, even carbons she'd made of some letters to doctors. She tells me I'm obsessed.)

I don't know if I'll ever show this to anyone. There are a couple of old friends that I wish could see it. Maybe Sally was right when she used to say in those cold, angry moments, "You're a coward, Phil." She said it when I wouldn't go for counseling, and she said it when I didn't back her up with Jackie the way she wanted me to. Perhaps I'm afraid my friends would say it to me too: "You're a coward, Phil."

When you adopt a child they tell you, "Talk to her about adoption early, so she gets used to the word. Bring it up from time to time. Think how terrible it would be if she heard it from someone else first." So that's what we did. Maybe we talked about it too much, and made her feel like an outsider.

But the trouble really started before that. I don't think Sally ever felt really comfortable with Jackie, even from the beginning. And I was too dense to realize that Sally was sending out serious distress signals. I thought an occasional pat on the back was all she needed. "Phil," she would say, "this baby doesn't love me." As I've said, Jackie was six months old when she came, and as far as I was concerned, she acted like any other baby. Sure, she was more irritable than Curt, our first adopted child, but I couldn't see that there was any real difficulty. She was a beautiful little blond with big blue eyes, and she had a wonderful smile when she was happy.

When Jackie came to us she was covered with diaper rash. I mean the rash may have started out where her diaper was, but it went up as far as her armpits and down to her knees—and she was scrawny-looking, and the smile I mentioned didn't really come that often. Sally thought she'd been neglected in the foster home.

Jackie got along O.K. with Curt when she was little, but when we were finally able to have a biological child and Laurie came along, all hell broke loose. Curt was seven then and Jackie was four. Looking back, I'd say that was when I began wondering myself about how normal Jackie was. We would find her in the baby's room, pinching her and making her cry. Once she poked her with a straight pin. But in other ways she was coming along fine; she learned to read early, before she entered first grade, and she seemed to know every child in the neighborhood. A lot of them liked her, too.

By the time she was seven or eight, she and Sally were always fighting. It got so bad I would stay at work longer than I had to, because I dreaded coming home to find them at each other every night. As soon as I came in the door, Sally would complain to me about some terrible thing that Jackie had done, or Jackie would say how mean Sally had been. I tried to love them both, but sometimes I felt like strangling one or the other just to get some peace. It's only now that I realize how badly I failed both of them.

Sally Whelan to Helen Simpson

February 14, 1968

Dear Mother,

We all enjoyed your visit. Now that Father is gone our family get-togethers don't seem as jolly as they used to. But I'm glad of one thing—he didn't see the turmoil that's been going on in my house. I'm sure you noticed the strain between Jackie and me, and were too tactful to comment on it. I blame myself, but I don't know what I'm doing wrong.

Our pediatrician thinks she might be hyperactive, and wants to put her on some kind of pills. I have real doubts about it—filling kids up with medication never seemed right to me. Somehow I feel that it's not her chemistry that's messed up, but the chemistry between her and me.

My job is going well. I'm earning top dollar for a legal secretary in Des Moines. Mr. Raiford wants me to work full time, and sometimes I'm tempted, but I keep reminding him (and myself) that my first priority is my home and family.

Phil and the kids send their love, as do I.

Sally

Helen Simpson to Sally Whelan

August 29, 1968

Dear Sally,

I just put Curt and Jackie on the plane. The stewardess was very nice, and promised to take good care of them.

It was great fun for me to show them the sights of San Antonio for a week. I wasn't sure I'd be up to it at the ripe old age of sixty-four. They liked the swimming pool best, naturally. And they both put away several dozen of Grandma's barbecued ribs. I made ribs *three times,* at their insistence. You'll accuse me of spoiling them—but isn't that a grandmother's privilege?

Curt was a perfect gentleman, held doors for me, etc., and told me a few of his jokes. (He's too young to know one doesn't tell off-color stories to one's grandma!) Jackie was an angel most of the time, too. I noticed that she wasn't as keen on making a good impression as Curt, though. Her things remained scattered on the bedroom floor, and she never volunteered to help in the house, though she lent a hand quickly when asked.

I tried to learn from her whether she has any particular "beefs" with you or Phil. Of course it's hard to talk to a child of that age about serious matters. The most I could find out was that (according to her) you make her clean her room every day. She also told me, bless her heart, that you "yell a lot." Who knows what to make of reports like that from an eight-year-old? I don't.

She's not an easy child, and I think you're doing as well as you can with her. I really can't think what I would do differently. Don't know if all this is any help, but I loved having them and feel ten years younger.

All my love,
Mother

Jacqueline Whelan, diary entry

December 25, 1969

Dear Diary,

The first thing I remember is my mother yeling at me for messing in my pants. I must of been around three. Ever since then it seems like my life is one long lectur. For being fresh, or messy, or "not haveing a relationship with anybody." I'm sick of it. What the HELL do they want from me?

It's Christmas and I'm ten years old and this is the first time I wrote in this new Diary that my aunt June got me. Do you think SHE got me anything? A bottle of toilet water is all—if you count *that*. It cost three dollars, she didn't even take the lable off. I knew I wasn't going to get anything, too—she told me when school started that I had to "change my attitude" if I wanted a nice Christmas. What atitude I said. And then she gave me this long lectur about how I didn't show my afection. What afection does *she* show *me* I wonder????

Jackie

Sally Whelan to Morris Scharfstein, M.D.

February 11, 1970

Dear Dr. Scharfstein,

I have tried to reach you by telephone a few times without success, so I thought I would write you a note.

You were recommended to me by a friend, Mrs.

LoPresti, who said you helped her son a great deal. I am at my wits' end with my adopted daughter, age ten. We got her at six months, but I seem to feel she has never really settled into our home.

In the last year she has been taking things from everyone in the family, has developed a foul mouth, and will not respond at all when her father and I talk to her. I fear for her future—hers, and ours.

I hope you can see us. Our phone number is 555-1619.

Sincerely yours,
Sally (Mrs. Philip) Whelan

Sally Whelan to Helen Simpson

May 29, 1970

Dear Mother,

We're all well here. I was sorry to hear about Aunt Sarah's pneumonia. I hope that's past history now and she's back to her round of activities—usually no one can keep up with her.

I've been working more hours lately and giving some time to the Garden Club. Partly it takes my mind off of home, sorry to say. Jacqueline is a constant problem: never does what she's told, never thinks of anyone but herself. I try to get Phil to help, but he really doesn't see the problem. I've even taken her to a psychiatrist, and he seems like a capable man, but I don't know whether Phil is going to cooperate with the doctor. I feel like I'm in this alone, and it makes me angry. The worst of it is, Jackie is mainly harming herself, and she doesn't seem to recognize it.

I keep trying to think what I did to her that was so terrible, and the only thing I can come up with is that I hoped she would love me from the beginning. The doctor helped me see that. I expected the same of Curt, but he was only six weeks old when he came, and with him things worked out fine. I see I was wrong now; Jackie must have needed more time.

They say it's nonsense, but once in a while I wonder if she could have inherited these traits from her natural parents. I don't like to think that way, but if it were true it would take *me* off the hook.

Stay well, and give our love to Aunt Sarah.

Sally

Jacqueline Whelan, diary entries

May 2, 1970

Hi Diary,

That last time I wrote in this book I was pretty mad. (Pist-off my friend Nina would say.) Actually Mom is nice sometimes. She made my favorit dinner last night. Spagheti and meatballs, and she let me make the sauce.

Jackie

July 16, 1970

Hi,

I wonder where my mother is. That's what I call my real mother in my mind—"mother" instead of "Mom." I saw someone on TV that looked like me and I thought, that could be her.

I'd like to see her, just to know she's all right. I don't know if I'd want to talk to her though. If I did I would ask why she gave me up. I'd be afraid I would cry or get mad. I wouldent want to get upset with her, at least not so she could see. Id want her to think I was doing fine, even if she did give me away. Who needs her?

Maybe I do.

Maybe she needs me.

I'm mixed up.

Jackie

October 14, 1971

Hi Diary,

Sometimes Mom can be so nice. I don't want to admit it but it's true. And Dad's usually nice. We had such a fantastic time at Lake Stanton this weekend. I even tried to help a few times. But Mom spoiled it in a way, by being so picky. And she's much worse with me than with the others. I told my friend Sam about it and he said that's the way parents are. But I think this is worse than what most kids get.

Jackie

Philip Whelan, journal entry

December 20, 1974

Sally contacted a psychiatrist who saw us for an hour together. Then he saw Jackie twice and spent an hour with Sally and another hour with me. He had an office with shelves full of toys, and gentle pictures on the walls. He recommended therapy for Jackie, and asked Sally and me to come in together once a week, "to support the treatment," as he put it. He was a kind man with a humorous smile, and he seemed to feel for us in our difficulty. I couldn't see why he wanted me there, though; I thought the trouble was all between my wife and my daughter. So after a few sessions I withdrew, saying I couldn't take the extra time away from the office.

Actually it was torture going in there and having to talk about myself, and how my father used to drink and beat on my mother and brother and me when I was a kid. I had pretty well buried all that stuff, and I'd be damned if I was going to drag it all out again. Let sleeping dogs lie, I thought. I would have had my old asthma and migraines back inside of two weeks.

Sally got bitter and accused me of sabotaging Jackie's therapy. She and Jackie kept going there for another six months, but nothing much resulted from it that I could see except that Sally and I were farther apart for a while. The doctor wrote to me once, but I never answered.

I used to take the kids out to give Sally a rest. I have to admit that Jackie could be a real pain sometimes, especially if I had to say no to her. But she could be a lot of fun too, and she liked to be "Daddy's girl." Come to think of it, I don't remember if I told Sally that I had trouble with Jackie outside the house.

Jacqueline Whelan to her parents

July 17, 1972

Dear Mom and Dad,

I love it here at camp. There's a beautiful lake where we swim every day and have boating. I wish you could have both come up. I think Mom would like it here. Will you both come on visiting weekend?

My cabin went on a hike yesterday. We had to get up at six and go bird-watching with this little dried-up lady named Mrs. Finch. She's named for a bird and she looks like one. By the time we were out half an hour she had seen about thirty birds and none of us had seen any, and we were all starved. Finally she said, "Who wants to see a purple-bellied sapsucker?" (or whatever it was). Everybody said, "Not me!" She got this sad look on her face. So I said I wanted to see it, I never saw one before, and she took me into the woods where there was all this poison ivy and showed me this little bird on a tree, while the others waited on the trail. Actually it was kind of nice, just her and me in the woods there for a while. But she was so square, the way she cared so much about a little bird.

I think about you and Curt and Laurie a lot. I hope things at home will be better after I get back. I'm going to try harder.

Love,
Jacqueline

Sally Whelan to Jacqueline Whelan

July 20, 1972

Dear Jackie,

We all enjoyed your last letter so much, especially the part about the bird walk.

I will certainly come up with Daddy and Laurie at visiting time. Luckily Curt's camp and yours have the same parents' weekend and you're only thirty miles from each other. We'll go there first, on Friday evening, and arrive at Camp Choctaw late Saturday afternoon.

Daddy and I liked your last sentence about trying harder. You really are a terrific gal when you want to be. I really hope, too, that it will go better between us when you're home, and I'll try not to jump down your throat about little things as I sometimes do.

I really loved the Polaroid snapshot you sent us. You look terrific in your camp shirt and shorts. Your hair is even blonder than usual, from the sun. But the smile is the best part. It reminded me of some of your old baby pictures, when you were just filled with delight at something. Some of your recent pictures show you with a brooding expression, and it was it was nice to see the smile this time. You really do have a beautiful face!

Love from all of us,
Mom

Curtis Whelan to his parents

July 22, 1972

Dear Mom and Dad,

Camp is going great so far. Some of my friends from last year are here, and I've made some new ones. I'll be going on a white-water canoe trip next week. We'll be gone six days.

Have you heard from Jackie? I hate to say it but partly why I'm so glad to be at camp is that home has been worse and worse lately. It seems like Jackie brings fights with her wherever she goes in the house. I wish there were something we could do.

How's Dad's garden? Any tomatoes yet? Say hi to Laurie for me and tell her I'll try to find a souvenir to bring home for her. It's kind of hard out here in the woods, but I'll think of something.

Love,
Curt

Sally Whelan to Helen Simpson

November 2, 1972

Dear Mother,

Sometimes, these days, I become filled with despair. Everything in our lives seems to be going well except Jacqueline, and I let her spoil it all for me. One month she writes us happy letters from camp, and the next she acts like a nasty little snip who couldn't care less whether I fix her dinner or sew up the torn skirts and blouses that she abuses every day. I don't understand what's happening to us. I'm sorry to unload all this on you, but no one else seems to want to listen. Phil can be so distant sometimes, and it's so hard to get through.

Sally

Helen Simpson to Sally Whelan

November 6, 1972

Dear Sally,

I have your sad letter here. It upset me greatly to hear of the continuing trouble with Jackie. Not that I thought everything was cleared up—far from it.

I wonder if there isn't some terrible misunderstanding somewhere. Couldn't that doctor get to the root of it? Jackie's not a bad child, surely, and yet you write as though she were out to get you. (She could be doing worse things than she is—drugs, drinking, sex. But I suppose that's small comfort.)

You were always hard on yourself, and denied yourself ordinary pleasures. I hate to see you having such a bad time. You and Phil should get away by yourselves this winter for a couple of weeks. Try to persuade him. I'll help foot the bill if necessary; it wouldn't be any hardship. And I'd be glad to come and watch the kids.

Remember, I'm in your corner all the time.

Love,
Mother

Jacqueline Whelan, diary entries

June 20, 1973

Dear Diary,

Today Mom got mad because I left my room in a mess (she says), then didn't clean it up as soon as I came home from school (I started to, before she began yelling at me), then I was rude to her. Why doesn't she ever yell at Curt? He's twice as messy as I am. I *hate* her sometimes, no matter how hard I try not to.

Jackie

August 31, 1973

Dear Diary,

I really don't know why I do some of the things I do. I never told Dr. Sharfsteen (spelling?) how much I think about my real mother. He never asked. It was always "You folks have a family problem." What about my other family? (If that's what you call it.)

Whenever I look at *this* mother I see her looking at me as if I was about to burn the house down or something. She looks at me with those big eyes, and the corners of her mouth turned down, as if *I* was *her* mother and I just spanked *her*. She never thinks I can do anything, but she never *lets* me do anything or *shows* me how to do anything. Daddy tries to help once in a while, but he's afraid Mom will get mad at him if he takes my side.

I wonder when all of this started?

I would like to see her do something besides look at me with that worried look. It drives me up a wall. I think she really believes I'm going to turn out rotten. I guess I *have* been rotten in some ways, but I'm just a kid. I don't think she thinks I can change.

Maybe if I did something really *bad,* I could find out whether she has any faith in me. The worst that could happen is they would give me up, like my other mother did. But I don't think they would do that.

Jackie

Philip Whelan, journal entry

December 20, 1974

Finally Jackie really blew things sky high. I can't understand what made her do such a thing—it was twenty times worse than anything she'd ever done before.

What she did was to take Sally's engagement ring and lose it. She stole some money too. Sally had left the ring on her dressing table while she and I played a game of tennis at the courts down the street. She'd left her purse there too. *A two-carat diamond*! We asked her if she'd seen the ring and she said, "Maybe," with a little smile on her face. I felt as angry at her then as Sally was. I wanted to shake her and bang her head against a wall. She finally told us, calm as anything, "I took it to see how it looked on my finger. Then I put it down somewhere and I guess I lost it."

We went through all her things. We went through the whole house. Finally Sally and I concluded that Jackie had done exactly what she said: she had lost the ring. Probably on purpose.

And what did she do with the money she stole? She seemed to want to keep track of it, because I found this accounting on her bureau:

Record of "Tommy" by The Who	$ 8.98
Makeup	14.53
Pizza and sodas with Sam, Ellie, and Bruce	8.50
Bubblegum (lots)	2.29
	$34.30

What we did then is hard for me even to write about. Sally was hysterical. She was convinced Jackie hated her guts and could never become a member of the family. . . .

Sally Whelan to Helen Simpson

February 19, 1974

Dear Mother,

You're going to think I'm the worst person in the world. But everyone else thinks it already, so I guess you might as well think it too.

Phil and I approached the Department of Public Welfare—where we got Jackie from the Adoption Unit—and told them we couldn't hack it anymore. She stole my engagement ring and "lost" it, with the diamond that took Phil two years to save up for.

The social worker looked at us as though we were crazy. She talked about therapy, and I said we'd already gone that route and it hadn't helped. She really persisted, and I broke down crying. I couldn't control myself. I must have said the most horrible things about Jackie. Finally she said we must all come in for interviews. We're waiting to see what will happen, but I really think it's best for everyone if Jackie doesn't stay here now. Maybe if she changes she could come back after a year or so, but I question whether she and I could ever work things out between us. It seems that all we ever do is hurt each other.

I hope you'll come to visit us for your birthday next month—though the atmosphere here is not exactly cheery.

Sally

Jackie Whelan to her parents

May 3, 1974

Dear Mother and Dad,

I like this foster home O.K., but it feels like a jail sometimes. I really wish I was back with you and Curt and Laurie. But I don't deserve it. I always thought I wasn't as good as all of you anyhow. Now I know I'm not.

I don't know if you'll believe this, but I wanted to make things better. I took the ring to see if Mom believed in me. I thought I could find out for sure, if I did something really horrible. I thought if Mom believed in me she would forgive me. I didn't really lose the ring. I still have it. I was going to give it back if Mom still acted like she loved me.

I guess it's better that I know she never did really love me. But I still wish I could be with you anyway. Do you think we could work it out?

It doesn't matter about the ring anymore. I'll give it to the social worker the next time I see her, and she can give it back to you. I never wore it.

Love,
Jackie

COMMENTARY
BONDING
DISRUPTION
HELP FOR TROUBLED FAMILIES

Adoption agencies have a name for what happened to Jacqueline and her parents. They call it a *disruption*. Hopelessly negative feelings can poison the relationship between biological children and their parents, too. But such a happening seems particularly sad when it affects an adoptive relationship which started out as an act of faith and love.

What can lead to such things?

To begin to understand it, we need to look at what some biologists and psychiatrists have called *bonding*.

People called *ethologists*, who study animal behavior, and other biologists who specialize in the behavior of monkeys and apes, have long been interested in how various animals learn to recognize their young and protect them, and what events can get in the way of a bond forming between an animal and its young. They have also studied the effects of depriving infant birds, monkeys, and other animals of contact with their mothers. They learned that the earlier the animal and its mother become acquainted with each other, the more likely it is that the mother will protect and nurture her baby; they also learned that without a protective and comforting tie to a mother, a young animal may become confused and attach itself to other kinds of animals; if it is completely deprived of a mothering figure, the young creature may show very disturbed behavior permanently, or it may sicken and die.

Psychiatrists studying human infants observed similar situations. Naturally they couldn't do experiments on babies by taking them away from their mothers; but when infants raised in orphanages were studied, it was found that the ones who were cared for and stimulated did well, while those who received only the bare necessities of food and clothing became ill.

More recently, psychiatrists have also observed mothers with their newborn babies, and found that some mother-infant pairs seemed to get along well from the start, while others did not seem to understand each other; the infants cried, and the mothers felt frustrated at not being able to fix their babies' distress. Other doctors learned that infants who were born prematurely, and spent the first few months of their lives in hospitals rather than at home, were much more likely to be badly treated by their parents in later years than were their brothers and sisters who were not premature. (Only a very small fraction of premature children were abused, but the fraction was considerably greater than what would have been expected for the general population of children.) This made the doctors think that some crucial connection had not been made, at a critical time, between those infants and their parents—a connection that would have protected the children from the abuse they later received.

All of this work has led to the idea that human beings share with animals the need to form bonds with each other. The idea of a bond between people is not a new or strange one; we feel bonds of affection with our relatives and bonds of friendship with our comrades. But the idea of a *critical period* for bonding between mother and child—a period when making connections is much easier than at any later time—was unfamiliar until scientists did the work referred to above.

Does this mean that no child will do well who is not raised by biological parents and taken home by them from the hospital as soon as the baby's fingers and toes have been counted?

Hardly.

It means, rather, that bonds between parents and children cannot be taken for granted, any more than those between husband and wife, or between friend and friend can—and that if a part of the early experiences that are usually shared by child and parents has been missed (because of adoption, or illness, or prematurity) then the parents have a special job to do, to try to tune their fiddle strings so that they're playing in harmony with their baby.

The tragedy of Jackie's story is that her mother knew from the first day that the music didn't sound right, but everyone else was tone-deaf, and no one knew how to help before it was too late.

What might have been the problem when Jackie joined her family at six months of age? We can guess something like the following.

Imagine a baby just old enough to recognize the main person caring for him—a mother or foster mother, probably. He's too young to say any words, and he's just learned to sit up by himself. This six-month-old has gradually made a wonderful discovery: he has learned that his caretaker is one person who has a certain face, a certain smell, and a certain voice. He has no sense of time, so from his point of view he has always known that this was his special person—just as from his point of view he has always been alive. There was never a time, he thinks (or would think, if such things occurred to him), when he wasn't there, and there was never a time when she wasn't there with him, caring for him.

Now, imagine that a social worker has found a permanent home for the baby. He's taken from the crib and room that he knows, and his caretaker kisses him and says goodbye, but he doesn't understand her words, or the tears she may be shedding. He's brought to a new place and held by a new person. He looks at her to find the familiar outline of the face he knows. He smells her, hoping for the familiar odor. He listens for the familiar voice.

He doesn't find them.

He's terrified.

He cries. . . .

Now picture it from the other side. A mother is waiting for her long-expected adopted baby. She has prepared the room well in advance; her husband has painted it the color she chose, and she has hung a pretty mobile over the crib and clown pictures on the walls. She finds the baby beautiful. She has not been warned that the baby may miss his former home.

Or perhaps she has, and she did not really listen; eager to make him her own, she might have preferred to believe that whatever experience a six-month-old baby has had is not important.

She holds the baby and looks into his face. He gazes at her, searches her eyes, and she begins to believe the two of them can be in love with each other as only mothers and babies can be.

Then his face splits in a fearful wail; his scream of alarm fills her ears, and she thinks, Already I have failed. . . .

This mother and baby may weather the storm. The woman may realize that it takes time to make a relationship. The baby, from his side, may be flexible and trusting enough to reward the woman with a smile before many days have passed. And so things may soon get better; usually they do.

But suppose the mother is a person who is easily hurt, and soon comes to think that the baby does not like her.

Or suppose the baby cannot adapt well to his new situation, and remains tense and irritable in spite of the woman's best attempts to soothe him.

And picture the possibility that the mother's husband, the adoptive father, cannot understand what is going on, and blames his wife for not loving the baby enough, or else fails to recognize that there is a problem at all.

Then you would have the ingredients for a disrupted adoption; perhaps it would surface a few months later with a tortured call to the social worker, or perhaps it would act like a continuing fire hidden from the world's eyes for years until it erupted like a volcano, scattering the debris of wounded lives.

The best treatment for this situation is obviously to prevent it from happening. (That's one reason agencies screen both the adoptive parents and the children, to try to make certain that no obviously unsuitable matches are made.) And the next best treatment is early detection. Pediatricians, nurses, and others who work with children are trained to detect signs of a poor "take" between an infant or young child and the mother or father, whether the child is adopted or not.

Many such situations *are* identified early, by professional people or by the parents themselves, and counseling is provided, either in the pediatrician's office or by a child psychiatrist, psychologist, or social worker. Helping parents and children to understand each other is an important part of the work of such people. The public is coming to understand more and more that family problems can be, and often need to be, brought to the kind of people who know most about them: people in the mental health professions, and sometimes pediatricians, nurses, and members of the clergy. They cannot work miracles, but they can often help substantially.

In the story, the psychiatrist could not help because he had two strikes against him. He also may have made a mistake. The two disadvantages were, first, that he wasn't consulted until Jackie was ten, when the unhealthy family patterns had already been operating for many years; and, second, the girl's father withdrew; he was afraid to face his part in the trouble, so he took no part in the treatment even though he respected the psychiatrist. He left his wife and daughter to fight with each other, when by staying he could have helped the therapist to bring them closer together. And if Jackie is accurate in her diary, the doctor may have neglected to explore her ideas about her first parents. It's hard to know whether it would have made much difference if he had done so, since the situation was so far gone; that detail in the story, though, shows that even smart and well-meaning experts sometimes don't realize how important these ideas and fantasies are to adopted kids.

Perhaps if all these factors had not come together in such an unfavorable way, there could have been a better outcome. As it is, Jackie and her parents will have to work out their destinies separately. The story is bleak as it stands, but we can hope that the worst part of these people's lives is already behind them.

LETTER TO AN UNKNOWN BABY

I've always liked the Spanish moss you see when you drive southeast toward the coast near Wilmington. It hangs from the big live oak trees that grow along Route 421. We used to drive from Durham to Raleigh, Linda and I, and catch sight of the State Capitol building, then drive over to the Interstate and go down it a short way till we hit 421. That would take us through Clinton, where there are some beautiful, big old houses, but once past there we found ourselves in pure farm country; alfalfa, hay, lots of corn. We passed black farmers and white farmers and they were all part of the land, no real difference between them.

Linda is a Tarheel, born nearby in Fayetteville, North Carolina, but I come from Pennsylvania and I'd never been in the South before. We met in a freshman English class at Duke, and for two years we saw each other pretty nearly every day, except during the summer. I don't see her much anymore, but I think about her all the time, and I hope she thinks about me. I want to marry her. But I don't know if she'll have me, after everything that happened.

As I was saying, we used to drive down to the coast on warm weekends in the spring and fall. Usually we'd go to Wrightsville Beach, since it was close, and sometimes we'd drive the extra hour across the South Carolina border to Myrtle Beach, where all the college kids go. But Wrightsville was quieter; we could get to know each other better there. We found a little boarding house that had two single rooms on the second floor. Linda wouldn't hear of any other arrangement (at least not at the beginning). They served breakfast on a glassed-in porch; I remember how hard Linda tried to get me to like grits with my eggs and sausage. I finally offered her a deal: "I'll have grits every morning for a week if you'll try eating your hamburger without mayonnaise." She gave up her campaign when I said that.

In spite of the grits, which tasted to me like something between Pablum and Cream of Wheat, the South had begun to grow on me. I liked the easy, informal way people had, and the fact that strangers greeted each other in the street. And when you left a store, you would generally be told, "Come back, now!" It was a promise of welcome.

I had never met anyone like Linda. She was quiet, and jolly, and shy, and confident, all at different times, so I never knew what to expect; she was always a surprise. But she stayed the same in one way. She was never mean, and never teased or put me or anyone else down. And (I forgot to mention) she was beautiful. Gray-green eyes, and a wonderful nose that I can't describe, and what the poets call a rosebud mouth.

Spring vacation of our freshman year I was invited to her house for a few days. Her father was vice president of a textile company, and they lived on a little street that was named for her family; I was so impressed I didn't know how to act. They took me with them to their private club, where there was swimming and tennis and a terrific restaurant; they gave me my first lesson in bridge, and introduced me to "pit barbecue"—to call it a pork sandwich would be like calling the *Mona Lisa* a picture. I was pretty anxious to be liked, and I used a lot of fancy manners and "sirs" and "ma'ams"; I convinced myself that they liked me, although I don't know how they could, considering how nervous I was. I thought they were terrific people—gentle, and soft-spoken, and it was fun to see Linda and her folks kid around with each other. My own relationship with my family was more strained. My parents had been having some problems getting along with each other, and when I went home they didn't seem like their old selves. So I felt some warmth in Fayetteville that I wasn't feeling at home just then.

That summer I worked in my father's printing business, mostly making deliveries, and Linda went to France with a tour group. I missed her badly, and in the fall I was relieved to see that she still felt the same about me.

We used to study together a lot, but we couldn't help each other with our courses much, since she was studying English and foreign languages and such, and I was in a pre-medical program with mostly sciences. She came North with me the first part of Christmas vacation and met my family. That went pretty well, too, and by now everybody—her parents, my parents, and all our friends—seemed to be assuming we'd get married after graduation. We'd talked about it a little, but we weren't quite at the point of committing ourselves to each other forever. We were only nineteen. That Christmas she gave me a sapphire tie tack that I still wear sometimes, even though nobody wears tie tacks anymore. I gave her a book of French poetry, a leather-bound imported edition.

When the spring began warming things up, our sophomore year, we used to go to the Mary B. Duke Gardens and sunbathe, or up to Lake Michie where we'd row around and do a little fishing. And when it got to be beach weather, off we'd go to Wrightsville.

We had said many times that we'd never go beyond heavy petting. We were both inexperienced, and I think both of us were afraid of "going all the way," as people used to say. But that spring we did make love a couple of times. We knew what we were doing, or at least we thought we did; we tried to time it to her menstrual cycle, but we didn't use any other protection. Those days we were on a cloud. The sand was sparkling white, the gulls and terns wheeled and cried in the sky, and we felt as though no one existed in the world but us; when we did notice other people, it seemed that they were all in a conspiracy to make us happy.

That second summer we were to be apart again: I was to work for my father, as before, to help pay my tuition, while Linda planned to stay in Fayetteville as a salaried companion to an elderly great-aunt of hers who was living alone in a large house. She would have done it for nothing; she loved her aunt, and it was in her nature to help people. But a week before classes ended, things changed quickly.

"Don," said Linda urgently as we met on West Campus late one morning, "we have to talk." She looked serious, worried, not like herself. I said, "Sure, let's go into the Student Union." We were just a stone's throw from the gothic union building, but she shook her head. "No, not here. Maybe we could drive downtown to the Jack Tar Hotel and go to the coffee shop there." I had a chemistry lecture coming up in ten minutes, but this sounded more important.

She wouldn't talk to me in the car; she stared straight ahead. I felt pretty tense by the time we parked on Main Street. The air conditioning was welcome as we settled into the wooden captain's chairs in the restaurant. I ordered the Brunswick stew with hush puppies, since it was time for lunch, but Linda just wanted iced tea. "Don," she began after what seemed like a year, "I missed my period. I didn't want to tell you until I was sure. But it was due eleven days ago, and I'm never this late." She had a tear on her cheek, and her eyes were full. I didn't know what to say for a moment; it was like Zeus or Hera or some other god had reached down from Mount Olympus and picked up the two of us by the scruff of our necks, between thumb and forefinger, and put us on a little stage to act out a drama. Suddenly I felt touched by reality and natural law in a way I never had since my canoe was swamped on a white-water trip when I was fourteen. There was no reasoning with the force of that current.

I reached over and grabbed her hand. "Lin, let's get married. I'm sure our parents would O.K. it. We wouldn't even have to tell them. We could just say we made up our minds in a hurry."

"Donald," she said looking at me sadly, "you're a big child." She extricated her hand. "Can you imagine that they wouldn't know what was going on? And what would happen to our status here at Duke? When was the last time you heard of an undergraduate getting married?"

Since then, I gather the policies have changed some, but at that time Linda was right. I suddenly realized that we would probably have to withdraw from the university if we wanted to marry and have the baby; we could have gone somewhere else, but it would mean leaving our friends and getting started all over again. But that seemed O.K. to me; I thought about Linda most of the time anyway, and I couldn't see why I shouldn't commit myself to her and the baby right then. Many people our age are married, I thought. I tried to persuade her, using all the arguments I could think of, and the hush puppies I had gotten to like so much in my two years in the South sat cold and neglected on my plate. But she said, "Don, it's no good. I've known people who got married that way; my sister's friend Alison did, and she was divorced after two years. Let's get out of here. I can't eat and neither can you."

We skipped our classes for the day, and went to the theater that showed foreign movies, where they were showing *La Strada,* with Anthony Quinn as the showman and Giulietta Masina as the innocent, big-eyed peasant girl. It had been my favorite film, but seeing it now made me feel awful; it seemed as though I were the cynical showman, taking advantage of poor, innocent Linda. Suddenly, while I sat there, nothing was right. I felt a reasonless anger at Lin for getting me into this: *she* should have used protection; it was *her* problem. And then I thought what a heel I was for thinking that, and squeezed her hand. And the thought occurred to me that there was a little pre-person inside her, something that might collect stamps or ski or cook or dance or laugh or sing one day, and tears started down my cheeks at the same instant that they did down Giulietta Masina's. Linda looked at me then, maybe from that sixth sense she has, and I could see she was crying, too. So there the three of us were in the chilly theater, all bawling silently.

She had a pregnancy test done and it came back positive; no surprises there. That night we talked for exactly three minutes about interrupting the pregnancy; she thought I wanted to do it, and I thought she did, and as soon as we got that straightened out, we hugged each other. No matter what else happened, no matter what our relationship to it was, we wanted that baby to live, to become a person.

At that point we had to think about telling our parents.

I had mental pictures of old cartoons in which the girl's father drives the young pair off his doorstep into the snow, shouting, "Never darken my door again!" while her mother stands there weeping but silent. I also had pictures of my own parents: my father telling me what a fool I was, and my mother muttering under her breath about how men are all the same. After several hours of such fantasies (which Linda was having too, in spades) we decided that the reality couldn't be any worse than the fantasy. So we each talked to our instructors, asking permission to delay final exams by a few days because of an emergency, and told Lin's parents we were coming to see them. Of course they would smell a rat immediately; they knew finals were coming up. In a way it couldn't have happened at a worse time, but in another way, the timing might give them the message, so that we wouldn't have to confront them with a complete surprise.

The visit to Fayetteville was hard, but not as hard as we feared, and more because of our own reactions than because of anything Linda's parents said. She felt she had brought shame to them, and I thought they would see through my college-boy pretensions to the worthless character I felt I was. We arrived in late morning, sat around the house in the afternoon, and then had dinner. Never, till I lie on my deathbed, will I forget what happened in her parents' living room that night.

Her father was sitting in a Windsor chair, smoking his pipe after dinner, and obviously waiting for me to make the first move; her mother sat reading nearby. "Mr. Collins," I began, "Linda and I have something pretty important to tell you and Mrs. Collins."

He looked at me; his wife looked up over the rims of her glasses.

"I'm afraid that I, that Linda, that we're pregnant."

I wanted very much at that moment to disappear and rematerialize in the worst salt mine in Siberia. Not only had I done a bad thing, but I had also just made a fool of myself, which for me was almost worse. I used to take myself pretty seriously. I looked at Linda for a split second and she had the ghost of a giggle on her face. I appealed to her with a tragic, betrayed look: she was mocking me. And then she and her father and mother, simultaneously, burst into the most raucous gargantuan hee-haw I ever heard. Their braying laughter made me rise, hurt and uncomprehending, and start to leave the room in shame and dismay. All at once Mr. Collins commanded:

"Donald, come here and sit down!"

I obeyed. I think I was afraid I'd be shot in the back if I didn't.

"Donald," he trumpeted, "congratulations; you're human like the rest of us. Martha and I have been wondering about that for the past year."

I gaped at him. He was no longer laughing, not even really smiling, but he had no hate in his eyes. I couldn't say a syllable.

Then I realized that Linda had not waited for me to tell her parents. Her trust in them, and theirs in her, were so strong that she had been able to talk to them on her own; they had waited for me to do what was right, but Lin had eased it for me instead of my easing it for her. I felt immense gratitude toward her, and great unworthiness.

The next thing that happened, if I'd seen it in a movie, would have seemed too corny for words. Mr. Collins asked us all to sit close together, and he began to pray:

"Merciful Father, we ask your guidance in the difficult

days ahead. Please guide us and our children to do what is best in Your sight. We are all children before You. Amen."

I heard myself echoing his *amen* along with Linda and her mother; I felt immensely comforted by Mr. Collins and by his God—I hadn't believed since I was six.

I felt absolutely no pressure from Linda's parents to marry her. It was agreed that I would fly home, talk to my family, and return in two days to Fayetteville. My father was somewhat better than I feared, and so was my mother. They seemed mainly concerned that I shouldn't "ruin my future," as they put it. "How can you finish college and go to medical school with that kind of responsibility?" my father asked. I couldn't argue with that; he had a point. But by talking strongly against marriage, they made me feel I had to avoid a terrible trap, when I wasn't feeling trapped by Linda or her parents at all. I did receive a modest offer of financial help, "whatever you decide to do," and for that I was grateful.

Back in Fayetteville I found that Linda had been thinking about placing the child through an adoption agency. She had it all planned: she would stay in her home town for the summer the way she'd intended, all the while telling her friends and the people at Duke that in September her parents were sending her to England for the school year "to broaden herself." I had to chuckle at that one. Then when the time came for classes to start she'd go out to Asheville, in the Smoky Mountains near the Tennessee border, where there was a Florence Crittenton Home, a place for unwed mothers to live while they were getting ready to have their babies. She had her parents' approval for this plan.

I hated the idea. My pride rebelled at the thought that I would not do the natural, right thing. I hated the idea of Linda living in hiding for most of a year. I felt cheated out of the gradual, calm deepening of my friendship and love for her. Perhaps most of all, I would lose that small person who was growing inside, who might have my black hair, or a little cleft in the chin like mine.

I told Linda, and she called me a baby. "You can't have it both ways, Don." She was telling me, without really saying it, that if I wanted it badly enough she would marry me.

But she wasn't asking, and I wasn't asking anymore either.

Junior year was the loneliest time I've ever experienced. I used to drive out to Asheville to see her almost every weekend, and I gave some information about myself to the people at the home, to be given to the adoptive parents so they would have some idea what I looked like, what I was interested in, what I planned for the future. It was a comfort to think that I'd be described as a "future doctor"; by that time I had convinced myself that those adoptive parents would only think of me and Linda as screwed-up, irresponsible kids. Linda was pleased with the way she was being treated, and the medical care was good. I found that she, too, was very concerned about what the adoptive parents would think. But her ideas went beyond that; as usual she was a step ahead of me.

"What about the baby, Don? What's he going to think about us? I have this feeling it's going to be a boy, with my gray-green eyes and your dark hair. But how can he ever know how we love him so much even before he's born? Will he ever look for us? And where will we be by that time? I'll probably be an old maid high school French teacher, and you'll probably be the most successful surgeon in Alaska or someplace, and we probably won't even be in touch with each other."

"I'm going to marry you, Lin."

But she was silent.

One fall weekend I took her over to Clingmans Dome in the National Park nearby and we had a picnic at the top. By that time she was showing her pregnancy clearly. People looked at us and smiled, and I knew they were thinking, *What a cute young married couple.* Linda told me she felt it, too. We looked at the land falling away below us on all sides, with peaks jutting up in the distance, separated by miles from our solitary dome. I said, "Lin, the mountains are cut off from each other. They can't talk to each other. Just like us and the baby." She nodded and leaned her wet cheek against my shoulder, and I held her there for a while.

Christmas was hard. Linda couldn't go home, and I had to be in Pennsylvania part of the time. But, in spite of family tradition, I resisted my family's urging to be home on Christmas Day. I felt I was growing up, and learning where my responsibilities lay. By this time Lin was very big. She had only five weeks before her due date. Her parents came out and took us to dinner at the Grove Park Inn, and we exchanged presents. Mr. Collins was full of good humor; I don't know how he managed it. He would have made a great general. Especially on the losing side.

The baby was due at the end of semester break. I went out to Asheville for the whole ten days of break. My two roommates knew the story, or else I'm sure they would have figured long since, with my frequent absences, that I'd either gotten involved in a smuggling ring or was being treated for cancer. They were good guys, and absolutely trustworthy with a secret. I had lived like a monk all year. My schedule was work all week, and out to the Smokies on weekends.

I found Linda in a blank, distracted mood. She was feeling the baby move around a lot of the time now, and she told me what a terrific strain it was to keep from having fantasies about him, or her. For example, she would feel a kick inside her belly, and her first thought was, This is bound to be a future football player for the Los Angeles Rams that I've got in here. And then she would mentally slap herself and think, I mustn't get into a relationship with this baby. I mustn't have dreams or wishes for it. I told her she was wrong, there was no harm in it, but she looked at me dry-eyed and said, "The baby's not inside of you, Don. When it's born and adopted, you won't be losing it the way I will." I didn't say anything. What could I say? I wouldn't be losing it the way she would, but I'd still be losing it, wouldn't I?

Her time came early on a Sunday morning. I took her to the hospital in Asheville; she knew the place well from having gotten her prenatal care there. I gave her a kiss on the cheek in the admitting area, and they whisked her off on a stretcher. I stood, and sat, and stood again in the waiting room on the O.B. floor; there were two other guys there, and I knew they'd be taking their kids home in a few days. One was a short fellow with a pot belly, and the other was a tall character with bad teeth. They had struck up a conversation and were comparing their wives' labor pains. They reminded me of Mutt and Jeff. I tried to smile back when they talked to me, but I wanted to knock them both through the wall.

I never saw my son. He was born six hours after Linda was admitted to the hospital; she told me they showed him to her for about two seconds, and wouldn't let her hold him, "because it wouldn't be good for you to get attached to him." While she was recovering in the maternity ward, I walked down the hall to the newborn nursery. It looked like a cross between a zoo and a supermarket. I figured I could get a glimpse of the kid somehow.

I looked through the plate-glass window and tried to make out the names on the little cards in the slots on the plastic bassinets: "Baby Boy Reilly," "Baby Girl Dlugacz,"

"Baby Boy Segal," and so forth, cute pink and blue cards, according to whether it was a boy or a girl. I figured ours would probably say *Collins* because we weren't married, but I looked for both names just to be sure. It was a little difficult because the only names I could make out clearly were the ones on the two short walls that were at right angles to the long wall containing the observation window. There were two whole long rows of babies whose tags I couldn't see: the ones on the far wall, too far away for me to read, and the ones right under the window, facing the wrong way.

When a nurse saw me peering up and down, she stuck her head out of the nursery door and asked if she could help. I explained that I wanted to see Linda Collins's baby and that I was the father; her smile turned to a cold stare in half a second and she said, "I'm sorry, that baby is being placed for adoption."

That burned me. Did she think I didn't know it? I went to the hospital administrator's office and waited for twenty minutes to see him. When I told him the situation, that I wanted to see my baby, he said words that chilled my spine.

"You call that baby yours, but legally you have no right to see him. And neither does Miss Collins since she signed him over to the Department of Public Welfare. I'm sorry, but there's nothing I can do to help."

"Not even to *see* him, man?" He couldn't have been over thirty; he might have been my older brother.

"Sorry." Like hell he was. He wouldn't even meet my eyes; he turned back to the papers on his desk. I punched a hole in his plasterboard wall on the way out—a small one, only about twelve by fourteen inches. He called a hospital guard as I walked out. (Cowardly son of a bitch, he could have run after me himself.) But I put on my reading glasses, combed my hair down over my forehead like some wimp in Latin IV, put on my jacket, and lost myself in the crowd in the cafeteria, killing ten minutes till it was safe to go back up to Lin. I figured they might not bother me there for Linda's sake, and they didn't.

Lin laughed when I told her about it. She really broke up. It seemed like months since I'd seen her laugh, and it was really good to see it. "Donald Price, you are somethin' else!" she exclaimed, and reached up so I would bend down and give her a kiss. I did, and called her a pet name I had for her, and told her how pretty she looked. It was the truth; she really looked beautiful then. And Lin whispered, real short and sweet, "I love you," looking me straight in the eyes. Then she turned away from me and burst out crying.

We spent some time that week drafting a letter to our son, to be kept by the agency in case he should ever try to find us; we told him of our love for him, and our strong feelings for each other, and a little about our interests and our families and what we hoped to do with our lives. What we had told the people in the home was for the new parents, but this was a personal letter, just for him. I said I planned to be a doctor, maybe a surgeon, and Linda told about her wish to teach English and foreign languages and to become a writer. We said we really didn't know if we would marry; we were both tired and wanted to be kids for just a little while longer. We signed it with our names and our parents' addresses, and gave the names of family members who could help him locate us in case our parents had moved or died.

Sending that letter felt to me the way I imagine those American scientists felt when they sent that metal plate out into space, with a picture of humans on it, and samples of music by Bach, and folk music, and mathematics, and specimens of a dozen human languages, so that many years later some unknown creatures might decipher it and read it and listen to it, and discover that the people of Earth weren't so bad or so stupid after all, and shouldn't be too harshly judged.

After the baby was gone things weren't the same. So much of our time, so many of our thoughts in the last nine months had been filled by the baby that it was a shock to know definitely, finally, that nothing we could do now would influence that child's life one iota.

Even the name we had picked out wouldn't stick to him. He would have been Marvin Collins Price. Now he probably had some transient identity, like "Baby John" or "Little Teddy," in a temporary foster home, where he'd stay a few weeks until some pediatrician pronounced him healthy and adoptable. And then he'd become some other couple's long-awaited little boy: a Smith, a Cohen, a Dembinski, a Russo. . . .

Linda had to finish out the year without returning to Duke if she wanted to keep her reputation. And there was no plausible reason for her to be in Fayetteville from February to June. So her parents had made plans for her to stay a couple of weeks longer at the Crittenton Home to regain her strength, and then go to the Sorbonne in Paris where she could improve her knowledge of French.

There was some practical value in Linda's actually going to Europe, since her friends and teachers might start wondering if they didn't get any overseas postcards from her. To Linda and her parents these things were important. I couldn't quite see the need for all the worry, but then I wasn't a girl, and I wasn't from a well-to-do Southern family. She could return to Fayetteville for the summer. Then she'd have to come back to Duke as a junior, while I'd be starting my senior year.

Even if money weren't a problem, there was no way for me to be with her and pass my courses for the year. Being pre-med, I'd chosen a biology major and had two tough lab courses plus statistics, history, and lit. My parents knew vaguely what was going on with Linda and the adoption, but they didn't know how emotionally involved I still was, and I couldn't conceive of their understanding if I wanted to drop out for the semester.

I tried to remember a line from a rock song that was popular that year—a Bob Dylan song called "The Times They Are A-Changin'," something about things being "beyond your control." That was how I felt. Briefly, that day in the Jack Tar restaurant when Linda told me she was pregnant, I'd felt that life was offering me adult status, if I could accept it, like the ring that kids on old-time carousels used to grab for. I'd really been sincere when I said I wanted to marry her. Then she'd discouraged me, and I hadn't gained enough confidence back to press the point. So I kept my safety as a pre-med student and I lost the chance to grasp the brass ring.

I tried to believe I'd done the more adult thing by keeping my career in mind. But here was Linda going off to Europe, and me unable to follow. How could we get back to the way we were at the start of sophomore year, with my second term classes about to start and only a couple of weekends to see her before there was an ocean between us?

We went out to dinner a few times, saw a couple of movies, and sat around in the Crittenton Home, but there was no privacy there. There was no privacy for us anywhere in Asheville. I tried to make things as jolly as I could, and I guess she tried, too. But she was moody at times, and when I talked about the future all she would say was "I don't know" or "Let's just enjoy ourselves tonight."

I wrote to Linda two or three times a week the whole time she was in Europe, and she wrote back, but less often.

Her letters puzzled me. She wrote a lot about the things she saw and did, but very little about us. When she finally returned and I visited her in Fayetteville just after my finals, I felt better.

We had a terrific weekend that seemed like old times. I took her to an Italian restaurant and then to a play; there was a summer stock theater in town and that night they were doing *The Rainmaker*. It was about a handsome stranger who arrived on a farm when there was a drought. He was basically a loser, but he persuaded people he could make it rain. I always have been soft-headed when it comes to movies and plays. By the time the third act started, I had myself identified with the rainmaker whose charm and male energy could make anything happen.

That was the night I proposed to Linda.

I'd proposed to her before, if you can call it that. Back in the Jack Tar Hotel, that day late in spring. It was impulsive, but I meant it when I said it. And yet I hadn't argued too hard when she brushed it aside. I guess my own life looked too scary if that M.D. degree didn't arrive right on schedule. Now, nine months and one baby later, I wanted to make it up to her.

This time I made an old-fashioned proposal. I told her how much she meant to me, and how I thought about her a dozen times a day. I pointed out my future earning ability and the interests we shared. I said we could be married in two years after her graduation and that wherever I wound up going to med school next year, I'd be back as often as I could to see her. But I didn't mention the baby, because I couldn't figure out how to fit a lost baby into a marriage proposal.

Linda listened and stroked my hand. She had tears in her eyes. "Don," she finally said, "I love you. You know I do. There's no one I care for more than I care for you.

But I don't know how to think about marriage now. I don't know how we could live together after what's happened."

I wasn't the rainmaker any more. I was a poor dumb Don Price, feeling the same way I'd felt since I was a kid: like I'd made a bad mistake that I didn't understand, and done a lot of damage that no one would explain, and there was no way I could ever feel better. No wonder I'd wanted to be the rainmaker instead. . . .

She went on, "It's not your fault, Don. When I think about it hard, I know perfectly well that what we did, we did together. But how can I say I want to marry you when every so often I feel like I hate you, and when I still cry a little every night about the baby? I don't know how it would work, really I don't."

That was two years ago. I still keep in touch with Linda. I graduated and started medical school in New York, and I've gotten to know a whole new bunch of people, but none of the girls here compares to her.

Next week the seniors will graduate at Duke. I plan to be there with a dozen red roses for Linda. We'll see what happens then.

COMMENTARY
BIRTH PARENTS AND THEIR DISTRESS
HOW PEOPLE COPE WITH PAIN
BIRTH PARENTS' REACTIONS TO THE SEARCH

The sadness of these two young people is obvious. They got into a situation they weren't ready for, and did the best they could with it, but it aged them and weighed on their shoulders. They were forced to choose between two alternatives, neither of which felt very good: to marry and take responsibility for a child while still in their teens, before they had prepared fully for their careers or completed the process of growing up, or to give up the child to an adoptive family which promised to care lovingly for it. A third alternative, that of ending the pregnancy, did not occur seriously either to Don or to Linda.

In some parts of the world the situation of these two people would not be such a tough one. Even in certain segments of American society a baby born "out of wedlock," as people call it when the parents are not married to each other, is not at any particular disadvantage, and neither are the parents. (Or perhaps I should say "the mother" here, because it has always been easier for fathers to avoid responsibility for a child, if they wish to do so, than for mothers. It's the mother, after all, who walks around pregnant for months, and who has to give birth.) Social arrangements in certain South Pacific islands are such that it is considered an honor to become the adoptive parent of a relative's child; and among working-class black people in the United States and elsewhere it is very common for the mother of an unmarried pregnant girl, or some other female relative, to raise the girl's baby as her own child.

You might ask, therefore, why Don and Linda have to go through such agony. To answer this we should first divide up their pain into its component parts.

First, there is the distress of having gone against custom by creating a pregnancy where there is no marriage—that is, a firm legal and affectional bond between two people—to receive and care for the child born from the pregnancy. Going against custom often causes people to be judged harshly, or to so judge themselves.

Second, there is the pain of having to choose an important course of action quickly. This is especially difficult because none of the alternatives is really good for these two people. If they marry, they lose growing-up time and can't follow through with their educations as they had planned them; if they don't, they lose the baby one way or another.

This leads to the third problem: that by choosing what they believe to be best for the baby, they cut themselves off from him, and him from them. This is perhaps the hardest part for Linda and Don, who both care about the infant.

Nowadays people like Linda and Don are referred to as birth parents, and in some places they have formed groups to talk about their experiences and to try to influence lawmakers to open birth records, so that they and the children they have placed for adoption can find each other later if they all desire it. But not all birth parents join such groups, even if they live in a place where one exists, and not all are in favor of opening birth records.

You might ask why they wouldn't all join. This question was addressed in the commentary on the first story. To look at it further we need to look at a broader question, one that has to do with how different people deal with painful feelings.

Let's choose one kind of experience that almost everybody knows about: the experience of losing in competition. It might be a baseball game or a wrestling match, or a spelling bee in school, try-outs for a part in the school play, or a contest in Scouts or the 4-H Club. For an adult, it might be amateur or professional sports, or the scramble for an important contract in business, or convincing the man or woman you love to marry you rather than somebody else, or beating out other people to be hired for the job you want very much.

If you've looked closely at how you and your friends behave when you lose in such a contest, you will have noticed that there are differences among people. (And differences, for that matter, in the ways people act when they win things, too—but that's not our concern right now.) One person might throw the bat down after striking out at an important point in a ball game and act mad at the world; one might shrug and say, "That's the breaks!" Another might get furious at the umpire or the pitcher, and still another might feel rotten inside but not let anybody know. And any of the stronger reactions might pass away quickly, or might linger and cause pain for hours, days, or weeks.

The same kinds of differences apply with adults who are in win-or-lose situations or at other important times in their lives. And the birth parents who place a child are no exception. For almost all of them, it's a painful experience, but they cope with the pain in various ways.

Some continue to cherish the idea that although they have given up the right to raise the child and be in close contact, they will one day have the pleasure of seeing the boy or girl they helped bring into the world and have some acquaintance with him or her. They take steps to try to bring this about—sometimes by writing letters to the agency which placed the child, in hopes that they will be sought out one day (like Don and Linda in the story), and a few more aggressively, by actually searching for the child themselves.

Some hope for such a meeting, but don't take any steps to make it happen, usually because they feel they should not intrude on the adoptee's life, but sometimes out of a feeling of unworthiness.

Some have such strong feelings about the whole process that the only way they can deal with it is by trying to blot it out, to make believe it never happened; these people are opposed to changes in the laws which would make it easier for their birth children to find them, since they are convinced that to meet them would bring back nothing but pain and would make their lives more complicated.

And finally, sad to say, there are people who simply don't care. The less said about them, the better.

When adoptees search for their birth parents, the reason their search has been called a perilous journey is not only because the search may be difficult, but because most of the time the adoptee has no way of knowing whether the birth mother or father, once found, will turn out to belong to one of the first two groups, and welcome the searcher warmly, or to one of the second two—in which case the searcher would suffer the pain of rejection.

But there are so many stories of birth parents published these days in newspapers and magazines, or presented on television programs, that it is easy to believe the majority of them feel a desire to see and to meet their birth children who have been adopted.

SUGGESTIONS FOR FURTHER READING

Much has been written about adoption, both fiction and nonfiction. Nevertheless, there are still not many good books for teenagers or younger readers that deal with the subject in a useful way.

One reason for this is that adoption used to be one of those things that people did not talk about easily. (As we've seen, that's still true to some extent.) Another reason is that adoption keeps changing, and a book about the experiences of a child who was adopted at two months might not be too interesting to someone who joined his or her adoptive family at the age of ten or twelve.

The reader should remember that adoption stories have been written for a long time; just take a look at the story of Moses in the first chapters of Exodus, in the Old Testament. And Oedipus, the subject of the famous Greek play *Oedipus Rex* by Sophocles, was adopted too.

I have included here a few of the best books I've come across. Works of fiction are simply listed, while I've added a brief description of nonfiction books. Your librarian can help you locate additional titles.

Fiction

Carter, Mary. *A Member of the Family.* New York: Doubleday, 1974. (For older teens and adults.)

Carter, Mary. *Tell Me My Name.* New York: Morrow, 1975. (For older teens and adults.)

Lifton, Betty Jean. *I'm Still Me.* New York: Bantam Books, 1982. (For teenagers.)

Miles, Miska. *Aaron's Door.* Boston: Little, Brown, 1977. (For pre-teens.)

Parker, Richard. *Second Hand Family.* New York: Bobbs-Merrill, 1965. (For pre-teens and teenagers.)

Terris, Susan. *Whirling Rainbows.* Garden City, New York: Doubleday, 1974. (For teens.)

Nonfiction

Benet, Mary Kathleen. *The Politics of Adoption.* New York: Free Press, 1976. Not only politics, but history and social customs, are described in this mature study of adoption in various parts of the world. (For older teenagers and adults.)

Du Prau, Jeanne. *Adoption: The Facts, Feelings, and Issues of a Double Heritage.* New York: Julian Messner, 1981. This is a very good book about how adoption got started in America, how it works now, and some of the present problems with it, including the open records controversy.

Kirk, H. David. *Shared Fate: A Theory of Adoption and Mental Health.* New York: Free Press, 1965. This adult book by a sociologist has had great influence in helping adoptive parents learn how to help their adopted children by first facing their own feelings about what it was like not to have their own biological children.

Krementz, Jill. *How It Feels to Be Adopted.* New York: Knopf, 1982. This book of photo essays lets nineteen adopted young people talk directly to the reader about their experiences. Photographs make the children and their families real to the reader.

Lifton, Betty Jean. *Lost and Found: The Adoption Experience.* New York: Dial Press, 1979. A thorough examination of the experiences of adoptees and, to some extent, of adoptive and birth parents. Deals with searching in detail.

Powledge, Fred. *So You're Adopted.* New York: Scribner's, 1982. A book for children about various aspects of adoption, including its history and the changes it has undergone over time.

Sorosky, Arthur D.; Baran, Annette; and Pannor, Ruben. *The Adoption Triangle.* New York: Doubleday-Anchor, 1979. A psychiatrist and two social workers who interviewed many adoptees, birth parents, and adoptive parents argue for more liberal access to birth records and describe the personal experiences of these three groups. (For older teenagers and adults.)

INDEX

Abortion, 43
Adolescent adoptees, 101–2
Adoption
  classroom family tree assignment, 69–88
  forms of, 11
  introduction to, 9–12
  kinds of, 9–10
  poor "take" between infant and parents, 139–62
  reading suggestions, 187–88
  search for birth parents, 13–45
  trans-racial, 89–107
  Vietnam orphan, 108–38
  wedlock baby (birth parents and their distress), 163–85
  when parents can't cope, 46–68
Adoption Triangle, The (Sorosky, Baran, and Pannor), 45

American Adoption Congress, 45

Baran, Annette, 45
Benet, Mary Kathleen, 45
Biological heritage, 37–39
Birth parents (and baby born out of wedlock), 181–82
Birth parents, search for, 13–45
  biological heritage, 37–39
  Chris's story, 13–36
  commentary, 37–45
  decision to search, 40–43
  keeping the barriers up, 43–44
  organizations for adoptees, 44–45
  relationships and, 42–43
Birth records
  access to, 38, 183
  open records, 43
Blacks, 86, 182

trans-racial adoptions, 89–107
Blended families, 10
Bonding, 157–61
 critical period, 159–60

Chicanos, 136
Child protective service (department of public welfare), 65
Children, protecting, 65–66
Classroom family tree assignment, 69–88
 awkward situations, 83–84
 commentary, 83–88
 fantasy, respect and disrespect, 84–85
 language problems, 85–88
 story of Jason McKay, 69–82
Competition, losing in, 183–84
Contraception, 43
Critical period (bonding between mother and child), 159–60
Cultural orphans, 135–37

Denial of difference attitude, 84
Denial of difference families, 41
Disruption, 157

Foster care arrangements, 39
Foster homes, 66

Haley, Alex, 135
Hispanic culture, 136
Homosexuals, 86

Identity, 103–04, 107, 134, 138
Kim Van Kieu, 111
Kirk, David, 41, 84

Language problems (or "knowing what to call things"), 85–88
Legal rights and privileges, 39
Lies, 40

Negative feelings (poor "take" between infant and parents), 139–62
 bonding relationship, 157–61
 commentary, 157–62
 disruption, 157
 help for families, 161–62
 Jacqueline's story, 139–56
New England Journal of Medicine, 97

Older children, 66–68

Pannor, Reuben, 45
Parents, meaning of, 87
Parents who can't cope, 46–68
 child-raising and, 62–64
 commentary, 62–68
 foster homes, 66
 Joanna and Kevin's story, 46–61
 older children, 66–68
 reporting to a child protective agency, 64–65
 second chance, 65
Politics of Adoption, The (Benet), 45
Powledge, Fred, 45
Psychiatrists, 64, 162
Puerto Ricans, 136

Relationships, 42–43
Reunion registries, 45
Rootless, feeling, 134–36
Roots (television program), 135

Schizophrenia, 64
Secrecy, 43–44
Social change and confusion, 86
Social customs, changes in, 10–11, 12
Social workers, 39, 107, 160, 161, 162
 concern for birth mothers secrecy, 43–44
Sorosky, Arthur D., 45
So You're Adopted (Powledge), 45

Teenagers, 101–03

Trans-racial adoptions, 89–107
  adolescent adoptees, 101–02
  commentary, 101–07
  identity, 103–04, 107
  Larry's story, 89–100
  opposition to, 107
  teenager, 101–03
Tu Fu (poet), 138

Vietnam orphan, 108–38
  commentary, 133–38
  cultural orphans, 135–37
  feeling of belonging, 133–34
  fitting in with adoptive parents, 134–35
  loyalty and identity, 137–38
  Van's story, 108–32

Wedlock baby (birth parents and their distress), 163–85
  choice of alternatives, 181
  commentary, 181–85
  coping with pain, 182
  reactions to opening birth record search, 181–85
  social customs and, 181–82
  story of Linda and Don, 163–80
Women, 86

ABOUT THE AUTHOR

Steven L. Nickman was born in New Jersey and attended Princeton University and Duke Medical School. He was trained first as a pediatrician and then as a psychiatrist. His interest in adoption arose from experience within his own family. He gradually developed a subspecialty within child psychiatry, dealing with the special worries and concerns of adopted children and teenagers and their parents. He has a private practice and is on the staff of the Massachusetts General Hospital in Boston; he also serves as medical director of the New Bedford Area Center for Human Services.

Dr. Nickman lives in Brookline, Massachusetts, with his wife and two sons, seventeen and eleven years old. He enjoys language study, travel, and music, and continues to write about adoption and other family-related subjects for both general readers and professionals in the mental health field.